THE MYSTIFYING MIND

THE MYSTIFYING MIND

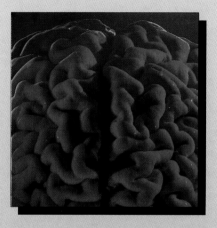

By the Editors of Time-Life Books

TIME-LIFE BOOKS, ALEXANDRIA, VIRGINIA

CONTENTS

A MYSTERIOUS ENTITY

The mind somehow straddles the physical domain of the brain and the abstract realm of thought, intelligence, and imagination. A mirror of external reality, it is not a rigid reflector, but pliant and vital, swept by ripples of life, emotion, and memory. It lives in the porridgelike tissues of the brain in somewhat the same way that incandescent light resides in a light bulb. But no one—no mind—has revealed how or where this mental illumination begins and ends.

Dealing with bodily functions, the relationship of brain and mind is clear: Commands go out as from a ship's bridge, causing the body to move, flinch, feed, and rest; the heart to thump; temper to flare; and all the other operations, conscious and reflexive, to proceed. A convincing case can be made that what humans call the mind is only the total electrochemical crackling of brain cells and circuits.

Yet there remains that other, mystifying entity, enigmatically self-aware, and the remote, perhaps unknowable, nether world of the unconscious. In these domains, the mind may hide its motives and desires from itself, and becomes capable of anything—high art and hope, despair and self-destruction, all the best and the worst of what is human.

Finding the Mind

Broken hearts and aching hearts are the stuff of many a lovelorn ballad, and none refers to a cardiovascular ailment. Rather, the hearts of song point metaphorically to the mysterious place where human emotions live. In so doing, the pained pumps echo ancient beliefs, set down as early as the fourth century BC, when the Greek philosopher Aristotle argued that the heart was the seat of all feelings and the home of the mind. However, Plato, Aristotle's one-time teacher, argued that consciousness is not found in the heart but in the brain.

The debate over the nature and location of consciousness is as old as philosophy and is still unresolved. Even if one pinpoints what consciousness is—an elusive matter to this day—there are still the baffling questions of why it exists, where it comes from, and where it goes. Philosophers of a theological bent have couched the issue in terms of the soul. For psychologists, the soul equates with consciousness, personality, or mind—the irreducible essence of a human being.

More than three centuries ago, the French mathematician René Descartes gave his opinion on what the mind is in words so crisp that they resound through Western thought today. In 1629, Descartes wrote that objective reality can be reduced to one phrase: *Cogito, ergo sum*—"I think, therefore I am." Descartes believed that the mind's peculiar ability to step back from its own thinking process was evidence of divine creation and provided a basis for a rational understanding of nature. Descartes considered the mind separate from the brain, a kind of master engineer who made the mental machinery run smoothly.

But during the eighteenth century, scientists became increasingly interested in the machinery itself and began to wonder if such an engineer was present after all. In Italy in 1791, Luigi Galvani discovered that body movement was not merely the mechani-

Although Plato (*upper right*) taught that the home of consciousness was the brain, his student Aristotle (*left*) placed the mind in the heart.

After Russian physiologist Ivan Pavlov *(right)* applied outside stimuli to train, or "condition," canine reflexes, American psychologist John B. Watson *(below, right)* boasted that any human mind could be shaped to order.

cal work of muscles but was controlled by electrical signals from the nervous system: The mind was an electrical entity *(pages 18-19)*. And, it appeared, consciousness could be altered by external forces. In 1902, the Russian physiologist Ivan Petrovich Pavlov showed that the minds of dogs could be "conditioned" with a well-timed sensory stimulus to change their behavior—by hearing a bell at mealtimes, for example, they became conditioned to salivate whenever they heard a bell. Around the discoveries of Pavlov and others grew an entire school of research called behaviorism, built on the notion that the mind was essentially neutral equipment that could be shaped by outside stimuli. "Give me a baby and my world to bring it up in," boasted American psychologist John B. Watson early in the century, "I'll make it a thief, a gunman, or a dopefiend. The possibility of shaping [the mind] in any direction is almost endless."

The preoccupation with the mind as part of a biological machine has led scientists to search for its physical location somewhere in the central nervous system. At different times, various parts of the brain were declared to be the mind's corporeal home.

Among the candidates were the small pineal gland that sits atop the brainstem, the gray cerebrum that makes up the outer bulk of the brain and is thought to be the site of associative thought, the limbic system in the deep central region of the brain, and the reticular, or netlike, formation that rests at the base of the skull. None of these, however, has quite filled the bill.

But new medical technology such as PET scans, which let scientists watch the mind in action *(pages 11-13)*, is spawning new theories about where the mind lives. PET scans, in the view of such neurologists as Richard Restak, are evidence that the human mind does not reside in any particular part of the brain but is rather the sum of functions performed by the brain's various components.

Not all scientists agree. The distinguished British neurosurgeon Wilder Penfield insisted that "the nature of the mind remains still a mystery that science has not solved." At the end of decades of medical practice, Penfield wrote in 1975, "I am forced to choose the proposition that our being is to be explained on the basis of two fundamental elements." One, the brain, is powered by electrical impulses; the other, the mind, derives its energy from unknown sources. Beyond that, however, he was as unable as his predecessors to explain the presence of the mind in the apparatus of the brain—what philosophers have called the ghost in the machine. □

French scholar René Descartes *(left)* equated being with thinking, a brain function later probed by electricity-minded researchers inspired by Luigi Galvani *(above)*.

Mechanical Minds

No one can say exactly what the mind *is*, but everyone seems to know what it is *like*. In the post-medieval era, the mind has most often been compared to a machine, as succeeding generations have tried to explain the mind with a mechanical metaphor from their own times—each analogue more complex than the last.

For René Descartes, the French philosopher of the seventeenth century, the brain and mind were like the mechanical statues in the garden of Saint Germain in Paris, where water-powered drives were built into the ground. When a visitor stepped on a tile, a valve would open and cause a statue to move. The system of pipes and valves, Descartes wrote, was like the sensory apparatus of the brain; the engineer who maintained the garden was like the mind.

A century later, the technical parallel was a clockwork system of gears and pulleys. Julien Offroy de la Mettrie, a French physician, wrote in 1747 that the "human body is a machine that winds its own springs—the living image of perpetual motion." In the age of steam, the mind became a steam engine. By the early twentieth century, when it became known that small electrical pulses are constantly moving through the brain, the cranial network was compared to a central telephone exchange. At its center was the chief operator who connected sensory inputs with their proper destinations.

During the industrial boom of the early twentieth century, some compared the mind to an executive

sitting at his desk in the brain. Receiving a message from the eyes, the manager sent the office boy out to recall a memory from the files, issued an order to the arm to shake hands, and told the vocal cords to say "hello."

Today, the most widely used mind metaphor is the digital computer. The British mathematician

A photomontage of watches superimposed on a portrait evokes the eighteenth-century view that the mind functions like a clock.

Alan Turing proposed in 1936 a machine that could process information as a series of "yes" and "no" switches, or "on" and "off" blips—like Morse code. John von Neumann built a computer on this principle in the 1940s, and biomedical researchers pointed out that neurons in the brain work the same way. They process information by firing (or not firing) an electrical pulse that is transmitted chemically across narrow gaps, the synapses, which separate individual brain cells.

The computer model of the mind caught on rapidly, leading to the field of research called artificial intelligence. It seeks to reduce the complexities of human thought to a string of on-and-off switches. But even the most sophisticated artificial brains have not yet begun to achieve the complexity of an insect's mind, let alone a human's *(page 14)*.

The age of lasers ushered in yet another metaphor: the holographic mind. A hologram is a three-dimensional image created when wave patterns from an undisturbed and a reflected beam of light—usually laser light—are combined. Like ripples spreading from two points on a pond's surface, the waves intersect to create distinctive patterns. A hologram "freezes" such patterns, which, left alone, constitute no obvious form. Illuminated by an identical beam of light, however, the frozen three-dimensional image reappears. Since a vast amount of information about the scene is recorded throughout the hologram, even a small chip from the original plate, if properly illuminated by a laser, can be used to reconstruct the whole. And holograms can be superimposed upon one another almost without limit—like thoughts, dreams, and memories.

This phenomenon, neurophysiologist Karl Pribram of Stanford has shown, bears a remarkable resemblance to the way the mind seems to function in the brain, where it appears to be both everywhere and nowhere at the same time. "Of course," Pribram has explained, "there are no laser beams or reference beams in the brain. I'm simply saying that our brains use a holographiclike code. The brain performs certain operations which can be described by the mathematics of holography, to code, decode, and recode sensory input. There is no other technique known to man that allows for the storage of so much information."

Instead of real images of a real world, in his view, the mind constructs reality from a complex mental counterpart of the hologram's interference wave patterns, derived from signals received from the eyes, ears, nose, and other sensory organs. Perhaps, as Pribram believes, the holographic brain is more than a metaphor. But history indicates that another, more fitting analogue waits in the devices of the future. □

Visibly Upset

Peering inside the human skull has always been a risky business—so risky, in fact, that for many centuries the only brains eligible for extensive medical study belonged to corpses. This situation eased considerably with the twentieth-century advent of x-ray cameras, which enabled doctors to catch a glimpse of the live brain without damaging it. Even so, x-ray technology involved injecting air or chemicals through the backbone into the cranial cavities to bring out structural contrast. The injections themselves posed a risk, one that sometimes outweighed the results, as when x-ray photographs were murky.

All this changed in the 1970s, when computers made possible several new kinds of machine—none of which requires a painful medical procedure. As a result, researchers have been able to look at the internal structure of the brain and watch the mind go about the routine business of thinking: reading words, making associations, and forming sentences.

The first new technique was computerized axial tomography, or CAT. CAT scans take fine x-ray images of the brain but add a third dimension of depth not available with conventional x-ray pictures. A more recent technology called magnetic resonance imaging, or MRI, provides similar three-dimensional cross sections of the brain by monitoring magnetic emissions of hydrogen atoms in the organ. But both CAT and MRI are mainly structural probes.

Positron emission tomography, or PET, offers a unique view of the mind in action—inside the ◊

brain. Such biological fuels as oxygen and glucose are tagged with a mildly radioactive substance, usually technetium. Then the PET scanner tracks the tagged substances from the bloodstream into the brain cells, where the substances are consumed. The shifting patterns of tagged nutrients create a second-by-second movie of the brain's blood flow and metabolism. The higher the metabolism, the harder that part of the brain is working; thus, PET scans can monitor levels of work being done by particular areas of the brain.

PET-scan pioneers seemed to confirm that people with mental

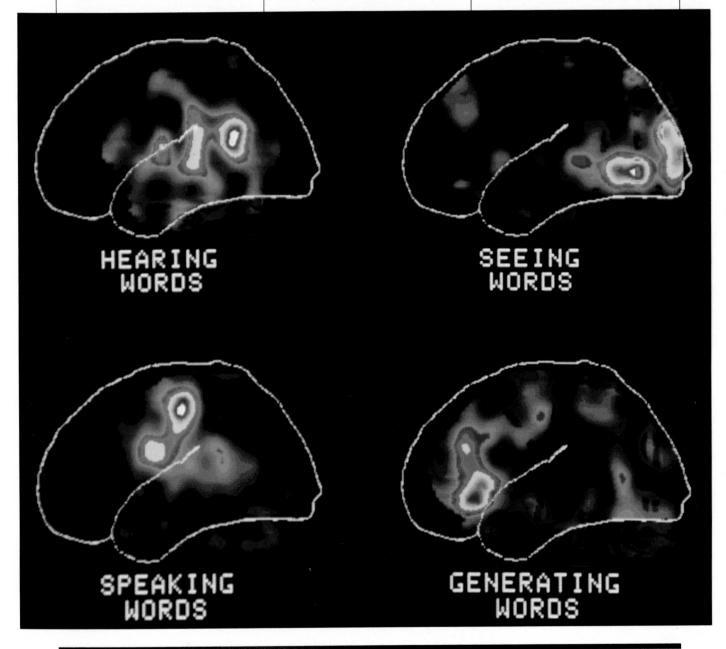

HEARING
WORDS

SEEING
WORDS

SPEAKING
WORDS

GENERATING
WORDS

disorders have physically different brains. In schizophrenics, for example, the frontal lobes, where future planning takes place, seem abnormally "lazy," revealing relatively little activity. On the other hand, obsessive-compulsive patients—those compelled to repeat odd rituals, such as endless hand washing—display abnormally high levels of activity in parts of their frontal lobes. The brains of sudden panic attack victims appear to be hyperactive; certain areas are constantly working overtime when a normal brain would be at rest—an excess of labor made graphic by technology that renders visible at least some of the hidden operations of the mind. □

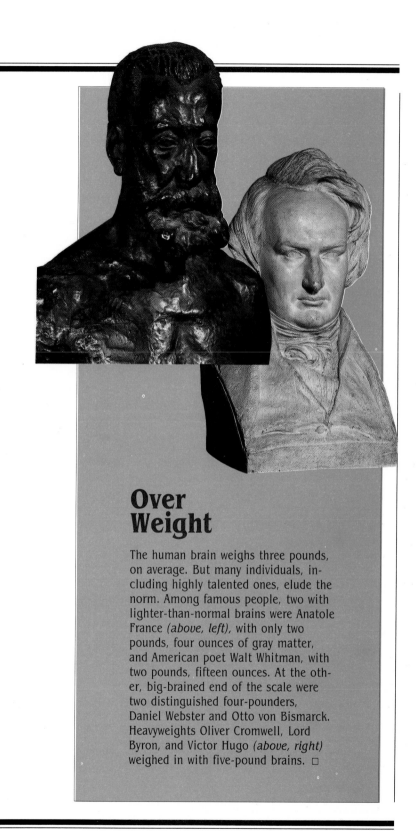

Positron emission tomography (PET) scans by researchers at Washington University Medical School in St. Louis show that different areas of the brain are most active (*indicated by white areas*) when the subject hears words, reads them, speaks them aloud, or thinks about using them in a sentence.

Over Weight

The human brain weighs three pounds, on average. But many individuals, including highly talented ones, elude the norm. Among famous people, two with lighter-than-normal brains were Anatole France *(above, left)*, with only two pounds, four ounces of gray matter, and American poet Walt Whitman, with two pounds, fifteen ounces. At the other, big-brained end of the scale were two distinguished four-pounders, Daniel Webster and Otto von Bismarck. Heavyweights Oliver Cromwell, Lord Byron, and Victor Hugo *(above, right)* weighed in with five-pound brains. □

The Uncomputer

For mechanical computers, the world is full of things that do not compute: contradictions, idle thoughts, daydreams. Science fiction teems with intelligent robots whose keenest desire is to understand the humor in human jokes. The famous Tin Man of Oz lamented his isolation from emotions and craved a heart. Machines cannot accommodate such subtle, seemingly wrongheaded qualities as irony and silliness, and have no idea how to play. For these and a myriad of other reasons, no thinking machines designed or envisioned approach the capable complexity of the human mind.

The computer is a logic device that uses electrical circuitry to carry out instructions fed in by switches and sensors. It is extremely fast in solving well-defined problems. It can sort through huge lists of alternatives to reach a targeted outcome in a flash. But the goal must be defined, for the computer will not stray from its instructions; it cannot improvise. Because it seems capable of digital thought, however, and because its signals, like the brain's, are electrical, the computer makes a tempting analogue for the mind. In fact, however, the mind is fundamentally quite different.

For one thing, it is alive. The neuronal cells that run the brain are themselves living creatures that must eat and survive in a wet environment, and they are affected by many subtle chemical influences, almost like fish in a sea. They respond to a variety of impulses. In contrast, the logic switches in a computer are made of rocklike silicon and experience only two modes of existence: on and off.

Human intelligence gets much of its information not from an orderly program but from the undefinable context of events. For example, if someone says in conversation, "He's bad," it can have two meanings. A person would know which was right, especially if the speaker was smiling. But on hearing these words, the computer would have to ask, "Do you mean bad (bad) or bad (good)?"

Unlike a machine, the mind exercises its power less by acquiring than by excluding information. Selectively filtering the flood of sensory inputs experienced every second, the mind ensures that only the relevant ones reach the level of consciousness. "Intelligent" computers are designed on the opposite principle, piling up one sensation after another to accumulate significance.

Finally, when part of the human brain is destroyed, the mind seeks to repair itself by recruiting undamaged areas and reallocating the mental work. In the computer, a loss of circuitry is usually devastating and must be repaired by a human agent.

Despite such differences, engineers persist in their attempts to build machines with minds. None has been very successful. One early effort was by Frank Rosenblatt of Cornell University, who built a complex device in 1960 called the perceptron. Connected to a large IBM computer, it succeeded in visually recognizing letters of the alphabet—but only if they were a certain size and typeface.

Since then, many artificial intelligence machines have been constructed. They play chess but cannot whip the world's grand masters. They diagnose diseases, run factories, build automobiles, but always with the aid of human physicians, managers, and engineers. Advanced machines may strain to process logic at speeds a genius could never achieve; but they cannot perform the first and simplest task of a six-month-old baby: recognizing mother's face.

Some researchers have tried to build computers that, like infants, are able to learn from experience. Gerald Edelman, a scientist at New York's Rockefeller University, has built Darwin III, a system modeled on the brain. It has 5,700 electronic neurons linked by 120,000 synapses, an "eye," and a four-jointed "arm"—all designed to sense and gain knowledge from a world that is not described by the computer program. In experiments, Darwin III exhibits behavior that is vaguely humanoid—observing, touching, and finally using its arm to swat away an object it has learned to find offensive. Sophisticated as Darwin III may seem, however, its rudimentary mind is far less intricate than an insect's.

On the other hand, Edelman says, the unassisted mind boggles when trying to study something as complicated as itself. "Suppose I understood everything about how the brain works," Edelman told a reporter in 1988, "I couldn't possibly visualize its processes. Just to count the connections in the cortex at one per second would take 32 million years. For brain theory, you need computers." □

Yellow-stained neurons, nerve cells that transmit electrochemical impulses, overlap with gray supporting glial cells in a microscopic wilderness of brain tissue.

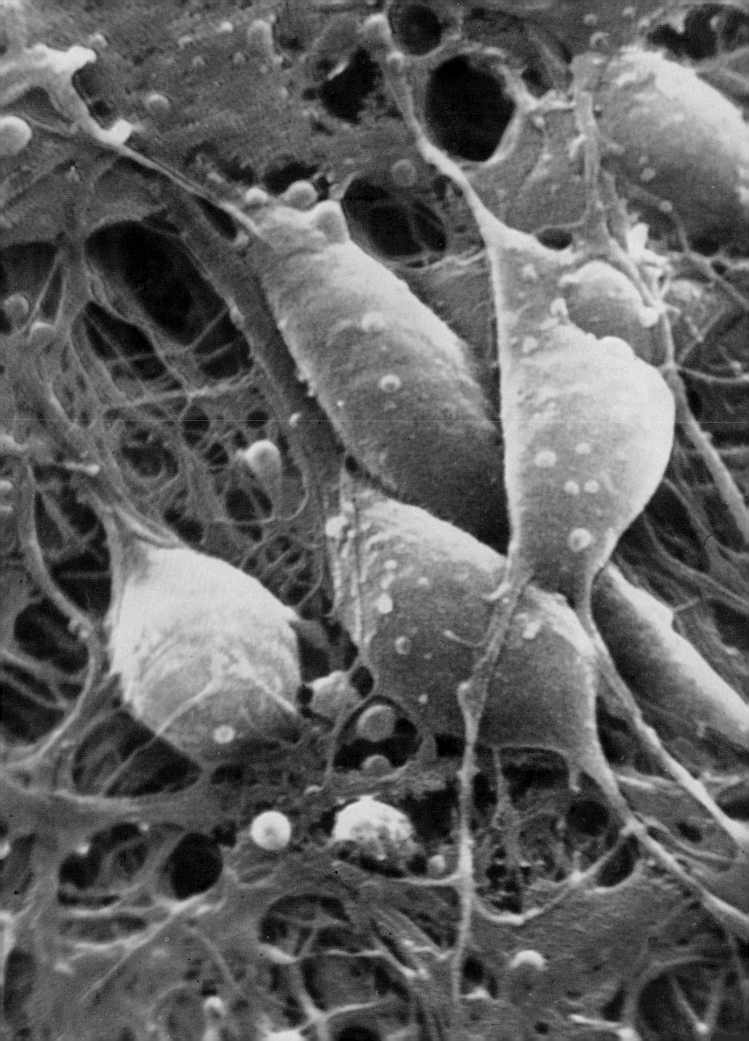

Mansion of the Mind

Most scientists regard the mind as the sum of activity in one of the body's largest organs: a spongy, three-pound marsh of tissue called the brain. Packed into the narrow confines of the skull, the brain is pinkish gray on the outside and yellowish ivory within, with the consistency of pudding. It is a porridge of some 10 billion nerve cells called neurons that transmit electrochemical signals across tiny gaps between cells: the synapses.

Without the blood that courses through the surrounding arteries, the brain would sag and flow. Indeed, researcher Paul MacLean finds it curious that scientists put such value on rigid, precise laboratory instruments when the organ that ultimately interprets the data is soft and shapeless. Though compact and formless, the brain possesses giant appetites: It continuously demands one-fifth of the total fuel consumed by the body.

Seen from above, the brain resembles a soft walnut. Its surface is bumpy and convoluted, its wrinkles providing an enormous surface area for the spread of neurons. The upper sphere is divided, from front to back, by a middle gap that creates two parallel hemispheres. Why nature favored this improbable division is not known; but all vertebrate brains have this double form, and the peculiar pattern of nerve linkage that comes with it. The left hemisphere controls the right visual field and the right side of the body, while the right hemisphere is tied to the opposite half of the body. In humans, the left brain usually controls speech—except in left-handed people, who often speak from the right side.

The two halves of the walnut, properly known as the cerebrum, are the most human part of the brain. The outer surface, the cerebral cortex, is the center for associative thought, language, and complex memory tasks. Particular areas of the cortex seem linked to specific activities or areas of the body, but much remains to be learned about how the linkage works—or how it works at any given time. Roles assigned within the cortex are not necessarily permanent because of a quality called plasticity.

After an injury to one area, other parts of the cortex are able to take on extra work and compensate for the loss. Without plasticity, cortex damage would be irreversible. Unlike most cells, neurons do not continue to form

after birth; the only way the brain can repair damage is to give existing cells new tasks. Young brains are more flexible in this way, in some cases even capable of switching the speech function from one hemisphere to the other after an injury. Adults are less resilient; when they lose the power of speech, it is usually gone forever.

The cortex, while crucial to humans, does not seem essential to survival. Animals that lose it—or are born without it, such as birds—get by adequately, although their behavior lacks flexibility. In fact, some humans seem to fare surprisingly well with only

Cerebrum and Cerebral Cortex

Corpus Callosum

Limbic System

This cross section splits the human brain in half, from front (*left*) to back, to expose cerebral components, which have been chemically stained to differentiate them.

a scrap of cortex, displaying normal intelligence and living normal lives *(page 54)*.

The two hemispheres of the cerebrum house the higher functions of mammals, including humans. Beneath this relatively modern addition are elements of the brain that are found in all vertebrates. The limbic system, along with such primitive areas as the thalamus and hypothalamus, controls the emotions and basic appetites: rage, the sex drive, despair, and feelings of hunger and satisfaction. This comparatively primitive region of the brain is filled with small bodies that are neither well understood nor structurally well defined.

Deeper still is the medulla, an area strongly affected by nicotine and morphine, which sends out the unconscious signals that regulate reflexive, or autonomic, activities: swallowing, breathing, vomiting, maintenance of blood pressure, and, in part, heartbeat. At the back of the brain and just below the cortex is another distinct segment, the cerebellum, or "small brain." It coordinates complex movements; ballet would be impossible without it.

Removing the cerebrum and cerebellum exposes the brainstem—the top end of the spinal cord as it enters the head. All neurons transmit their messages along long fibers called axons and receive on branching fibers called dendrites. But in this butterfly-shaped cord, the neurons are the largest cells in the body, with extraordinarily long—some more than three feet long—axons that carry signals to the muscles, the skin, and the brain. The backbone is packed not only with these extended axons but also with cerebrospinal fluid—a clear liquid akin to blood but lacking red or white cells. It fills a central canal in the spinal column and cavities (the ventricles) in the skull, keeping the brain bathed in a nutritive bath of oxygen and glucose.

At the brain's most rudimentary level of nervous response, nerves in the spinal cord collect sensations from the body and retransmit action messages to the muscles. For example, the doctor's familiar hammer tap on the knee sends a signal to a nerve in the spine, where an instant reflex is generated, causing the leg to jerk. However, a more complex sensation such as heat must travel all the way up the spine to the brainstem, where, after a slight delay, an unconscious response travels back down the spine and out to the muscle before it triggers action.

Conscious actions require the most apparatus. They must be filtered through the sophisticated cerebrum—perhaps to pull information from memory or to weigh alternative courses of behavior—before the signal to act comes back down the spinal column. It is in this field of effort that the human brain excels. This is also its slowest arena, as illustrated by the pace, for example, of a chess match. Conscious thought differs from other forms of nerve stimulation in that it is confined entirely to the brain. Signals ping back and forth within the skull, transmitting information around the "associative areas" of the cortex until the process reaches a stage at which the mind must decide what action should be taken. After all that pinging, often as not, the final decision is to do nothing at all. □

Although complex, the human brain is unrivaled in efficiency. A man-made electronic device with an equivalent computing power would climb a hundred stories above ground and cover an area the size of the state of Texas.

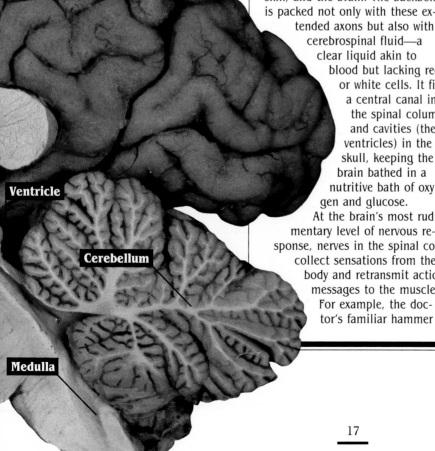

Ventricle

Cerebellum

Medulla

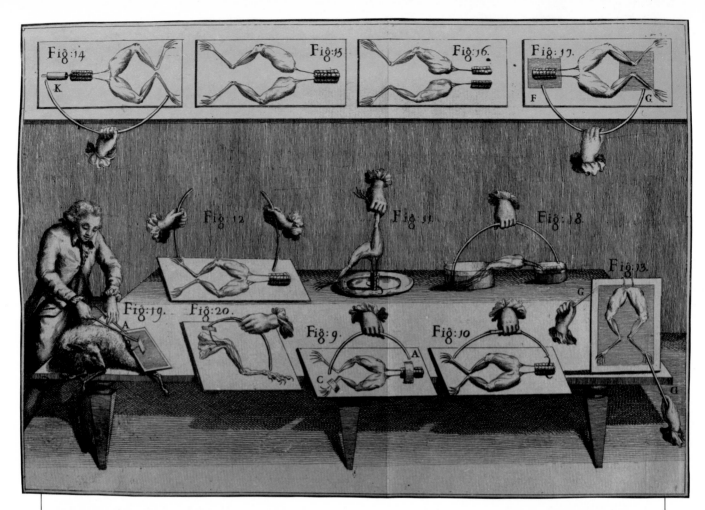

Impulsive Behavior

It had been known since the days of Luigi Galvani in the 1700s that electricity—what he called "animal electricity"—played an important role in the body. Galvani, an Italian anatomist, discovered what has since been named the galvanic reflex after he left dissected frogs on brass hooks in his lab. A thunderstorm passed by, and its static electricity made the dead frogs twitch. This suggested that electrical currents in the body caused muscles to contract. But no one could quite work out how the current was generated or transmitted. A century and a half after Galvani and the frogs, two British scientists used another lowly creature—a squid—to offer an explanation.

The sea squid provided the first direct insight into what goes on in the nervous system. The squid has a thick nerve cell running the length of its tubular body, an axon several times thicker than any nerve in humans. Researchers Alan Hodgkin and Andrew Huxley realized in 1939 that the squid's axon—unlike those in other animals—was wide enough to instrument with electrodes. Attaching probes to the creature, Hodgkin and Huxley discovered how its bioelectric circuits worked.

Nerve fibers such as those in the squid and frog crisscross every part of the brain and extend from the head through the spine to the farthest parts of the body. Electrical impulses can be created anywhere along the fiber (or in the brain) by disturbing the electrical balance between negatively charged chemicals, or ions, inside the neuron, and a positive electrical charge on its outer surface. Stimulation of the outer surface generates a signal that is passed along the axon. In the squid and the frog—and in humans—the brain sends messages this way to the rest of the body, and the body sends signals back.

There are billions of nerve cells in the human brain—nobody knows exactly how many—and each one of them has thousands of links to other neurons. The signals must cross from one nerve cell to another through an interface area, given the name synapse by turn-of-the-century English physiologist Charles Sherrington. Before the advent of the electron microscope, the arrangement of neurons suggested a junction box or vast telephone switchboard, with everything connected to everything else. This was exactly how many scientists long regarded the brain. But electric box imagery failed to explain the synapses, which powerful microscopes soon revealed to be not connections but tiny gaps—not circuits but circuit breakers.

Scientists now know that, to complete the transmission across the microscopically small synapses, an elaborate chemical transformation is required. When an electric signal arrives at the end of a nerve fiber, it causes tiny chemical packets to be released by the nerve cell into the synapse. There are forty to fifty of these chemicals, called neurotransmitters, brewed to excite or inhibit action. A single event sends many of them flooding into the synapses. The brain's task is to sort and weigh this chemistry, coming up with a set of sensible but explicit instructions for the body. On the far shore of the synapse, the message is reconstituted as an electrical impulse and sent on its way.

The complex electrochemistry of thought involves sending and resending signals back and forth within the brain, triggering complex memories and associations. It is an energy-intensive kind of labor, requiring enormous quantities of fuel in the form of glucose and oxygen. But, compared to any other thinking apparatus, even the most brilliant mind is a model of efficiency. Working at maximum power, the brain consumes no more than twenty watts of power— about as much as a refrigerator light bulb. Despite the much-vaunted speed of thought, however, none of this happens very quickly. The mind's fastest signals travel at only some 200 miles per hour, and many creep along at 55. □

The brain has been compared to an electric junction box—an oversimplification, of course. But if an electrician were needed to wire up all the neurons in the human skull, the job would never get done. Even soldering connections at the impossible pace of one per second, the electrician would need more than 30 million years to finish.

Brainstorms

Historically, epilepsy has been regarded with awe or alarm or both—for understandable reasons. The causes cannot be seen, it comes at unpredictable moments, and in its severe form it triggers convulsions and startling behavior.

Moments before a major attack, an epileptic may sense an approaching aura of sounds and colors. Often the onset prompts a brief cry. The muscles first go rigid, then begin to shake uncontrollably. The fit passes in a few minutes as suddenly as it came, usually doing no physical harm. Afterward, the epileptic may remember nothing of what happened, although some victims recall having strange and memorable visions during the seizure.

The ancient Greeks called epilepsy "the sacred disease" because the mutterings of seizure victims were taken to be prophetic. Medieval people thought epileptics were possessed by demons and inflicted supposed cures that were as cruel as the disorder. Often a hole was bored in the skull to let the evil spirits out. Sometimes victims were simply banished, like lepers.

By the 1800s, however, magic had given way to science, and doctors had begun searching for epilepsy's cause and cure. In the 1860s, British physician Sir Samuel Wilks gave patients bromides to prevent seizures. In 1912, barbiturates began to be used as a defense against the debilitating fits.

But the real breakthrough did not come until 1929, when German psychiatrist Hans Berger invented a machine that made tracings of electric brain pulses. The tracings were called electroencephalograms—EEGs. These "strange little pictures consisting of nothing but wavy lines," as one scientist called them, opened a new door into the mind and into the understanding of epilepsy.

Analysis of these brain waves revealed four main types, classed by frequency (the number of oscillations per second): alpha waves, at eight to thirteen cycles per second, typical of the adult mind at rest; faster beta waves, with frequencies up to thirty cycles per second, related to the areas of the brain that coordinate movement; longer delta waves, at one to three cycles per second, common in deep sleep, infancy, and cases involving a brain tumor; and theta waves, at four to seven cycles per second, seen in drowsiness and in light sleep. Ordinarily, the brain emits only one type of wave at a time. ◊

Any one of the four types of waves can be affected by an epileptic episode. The normally smooth and steady wave pattern gives way to jagged leaps of energy, signaling an electrical storm that sweeps across part or all of the brain. Experiments have shown that the storm can sometimes be set off by a sudden stimulus—such as a blinking light or a ringing bell— that somehow causes the epileptic's brain to lose its ability to control the firing of neurons. Apparently devoid of control, large groups of nerve cells fire together, convulsively, and the mind is lost in electrical turbulence.

Today, epilepsy is known to be a fairly common disorder, afflicting about two percent of the population, or four million people in the United States alone. It has been classified into a half-dozen categories, including these major groups: grand mal (the rigid and shaking behavior that lasts a few minutes), status epilepticus (a more dangerous form that can last hours), petit mal (a short and mild version, often noticeable only as a blank expression), akinetic seizures (limpness), and focal seizures (those localized in a small part of the brain and hard to identify). With the advent of such modern

anticonvulsant drugs as Dilantin, epilepsy is usually controllable.

But why some suffer these mental cataclysms and others do not remains a mystery. Animal studies have produced a theory that epileptic brains are perhaps too efficient in communicating nerve signals. A strong stimulus, instead of triggering a cascade of thoughts, sends the mind into a pulsating burst of electrical discharges. Perhaps, some researchers theorize, the very feature that makes the human mind superior—the electrochemical interlinking of many parts of the brain—may simply be overdeveloped in the epileptic. □

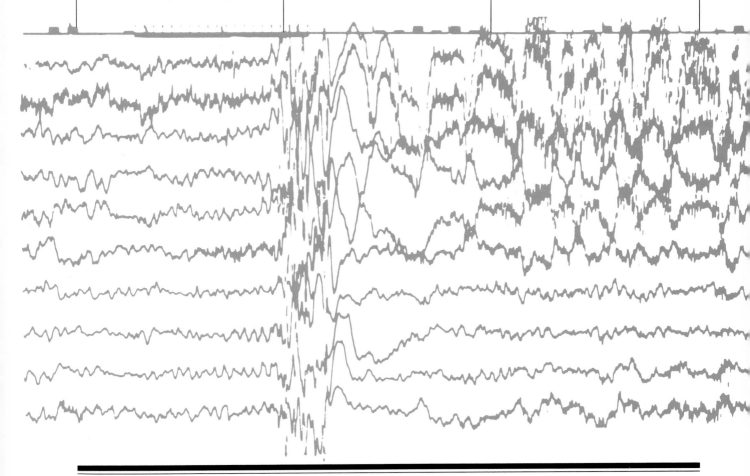

Electroencephalogram (EEG) measurements at ten skull locations show the normal, regular pattern of brain activity *(left)* **replaced by the erratic waves of an epileptic seizure.**

Self-Help

Captain David Tumey and a trio of civilian scientists have created one of the world's weirdest aircraft cockpits at the Wright-Patterson Air Force Base in Dayton, Ohio. In it, a pilot "flies" a simulated fighter plane without touching the controls. He steers instead with his mind by sending brain waves to a computer through electrodes attached to his head. The pilot watches a fluorescent light that has been slowed from the normal 60 fluctuations per second to a flickering 13.5. The brain uses the light as a mental metronome. By synchronizing with the light, the pilot chooses a right turn. When he lets his brain drift out of synchronization, the electronic airplane turns left. Level flight is achieved somewhere in between.

Tumey himself has become skilled in the technique. For example, he can cause the simulator cockpit, which rests on an electrically powered axle, to go into a steep forty-five-degree banked turn in less than a second.

The mind-flown simulator uses a technique called biofeedback, first explored in the late 1960s by such pioneers as Veterans Administration biochemist Barbara Brown of Sepulveda, California. In her laboratory, wires were attached to a subject's head to measure electrical activity, and the output was displayed as colored lights for the person to observe. Subjects then learned by trial and error to change their alpha wave patterns. Then, as now, the most successful learners said they did not understand exactly what they were doing; they simply practiced until they

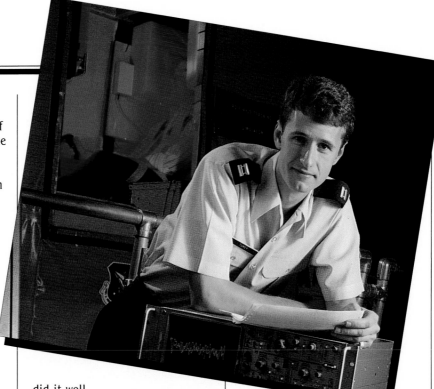

did it well.

After Brown's success with alpha waves, researchers wanted to see if body functions might be controlled through biofeedback. Experiments with rats suggested that they could be trained to change heart rate, blood pressure, body temperature, and even urine formation. In the 1970s, several labs also reported that humans had used biofeedback to control the rate of blood flow to the hands and feet. This hinted that there might be Western, scientific sense in the claims of Eastern yogis, who are said to be able to regulate their own body temperature, pulse rate, and other supposedly involuntary body functions by mental discipline.

The ability to control blood circulation—in particular, to combat the ailment called Raynaud's disease—is now probably the best established medical use of biofeedback. Raynaud's sufferers (most of them women) have poor circulation in the extremities; in chilly weather their hands turn a mottled

Biofeedback, traditionally used for relaxation and special therapy, has found a new application in Air Force Captain David Tumey's mind-guided flight simulator, shown at rear.

blue and pink and grow painfully cold. Keith Sedlacek of the Stress Regulation Institute of New York has been training Raynaud's sufferers for fourteen years in the use of biofeedback methods and claims that 80 percent of them have learned to relieve their discomfort with regular exercises. The clients learn soothing mental routines that cause the blood vessels to relax, dilate, and transport more warming blood to the extremities.

Biofeedback therapy has also become common in many other fields. It is being used to reduce blood pressure and stress, help nerve-damaged people reestablish links between the brain and paralyzed limbs, control stress-related pain, and teach Shuttle astronauts how to avoid space sickness. □

Severed Heads

Few took notice in 1836 when a country doctor named Marc Dax presented a revolutionary theory about human intelligence at a medical gathering in Montpellier, France. His claim, after observing patients over many years, was that most people who lost speech after some physical damage—more than forty in his practice—had a defect on the left side of the brain. But he had never seen anyone lose speech after damage to the right side. Dax's conclusion: The capacity for language had some special relation to the left side of the brain. Dax's finding, ignored for a quarter-century, was rediscovered independently in 1861 by Parisian surgeon Paul Broca. More than a century of research since then has proved Broca and Dax essentially correct, both in what they observed and in what the observations implied: Certain brain functions appear to be segregated on one side of the brain or the other.

Research clearly shows, for example, that the left brain excels in handling sequential and analytical information, in addition to spoken and written words. By comparison, the right brain seems more adept at identifying geometrical shapes, connecting faces with names, and controlling musical performance and tone of voice.

Unfortunately, isolating only a few hard facts about the brain's division of labor has led to the somewhat exaggerated notion that people have what amounts to two separate intellects—a left brain and a right brain. Speculation has it, for instance, that the right brain is the home of intuition and inspiration and, perhaps because it is usually mute, that it is underutilized. As a result, mental self-help recipes today often cite enhanced "right-brainedness" as a path to greater personal achievement.

Some researchers see this lateral difference between hemispheres almost as two different people in every single mind: a logical left-brain type and an intuitive right-brain character. Often, one side appears to be more influential than the other. In popular theories, this idea has been extended to create the belief that an articulate, logical person is dominated by the left side of the brain, while a metaphor-making mystic is ruled by the right. Entire cultures have been categorized in this way: Europe and America are said to be left brain, and most of Asia, right.

But more recent studies suggest that, while definitely different, the hemispheres may be less at odds than they seem. Among the experts holding this revised view are Marcel Kinsbourne of Harvard Medical School and his colleague Merrill Hiscock of the University of Houston. The two neuropsychologists conclude that "reasoning and logic have never been shown to be represented in one hemisphere, nor indeed, has creative thinking." In fact, they say, people use both hemispheres all the time; the two are clearly complementary, and in case of damage, each can compensate for the other. For example, although verbal expression is known to be centered in the left hemisphere, the right hemisphere helps shape the thoughts expressed. Sometimes, when the left has been silenced, the right brain will begin to speak. "Popular claims regarding fundamental differences between how people use the hemispheres," says Kinsbourne, "are without empirical basis." □

Audio in Utero

A fetus can hear sounds even while awaiting birth in its mother's womb; this has been known for some time. A loud sound often causes the unborn child to give a kick of concern or protest. But new research indicates that fetuses can do more than merely hear: They can distinguish one sound from another. According to University of North Carolina researcher Anthony J. DeCasper, the unborn are listening and even paying attention.

Psychologist DeCasper reached these conclusions using a sensor he had invented—a "non-nutritive nipple" attached to a sound recording device. He measured the rate and intensity of a newborn's sucking patterns. Then he arranged to have a recorder play back different tapes, as determined by the child's sucking behavior. Fewer than seventy-two hours after birth, the babies consistently chose to listen to their own mother's voice.

DeCasper also asked a group of sixteen pregnant women to read *The Cat in the Hat* aloud during the final six and a half weeks of their pregnancy. In this way, each fetus got to hear the classic Dr. Seuss story for five hours. After birth, the babies were given De- Casper's electronic nipple and allowed to suck select either a recording of mother reading *The Cat in the Hat* or *The King, the Mice and the Cheese*, a rhyming children's story by Nancy and Eric Gurney with a very different meter. The overwhelming majority opted for *The Cat in the Hat*. Of course, one study can yield no absolute conclusions about mentalities of the unborn. Nevertheless, DeCasper inferred from his work that some babies can—and do—acquire in utero a taste for Dr. Seuss. □

This newborn sucks harder on a non-nutritive nipple when she hears a recording of *The Cat in the Hat* than she does in response to another rhyming story, suggesting a preference evidently acquired in utero.

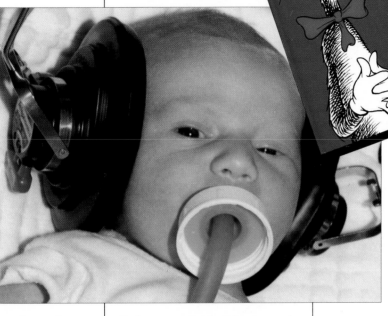

THE CAT IN THE HAT

I CAN READ IT ALL BY MYSELF
Beginner Books

By **Dr. Seuss**

In 1897, California psychologist G. M. Stratton tested the adaptability of the human mind with a pair of homemade goggles. The lenses turned the world upside down and backward. After putting them on, Stratton stumbled about in dreamy confusion for a few days but gradually learned to go about his business as usual. When he later removed the goggles, he stumbled about again for a short time, until his mind readjusted to the normal world.

Time Out of Mind

A child is born with a lot of gray matter, as the substance of the brain is often called—about twelve ounces, on average. Like a sculptor's granite block, the infant brain has more material than it needs—somewhere between 50 billion and 100 billion nerve cells, or neurons. As the brain matures, it increases in weight to about three pounds. However, it loses all but some 10 billion neurons, each linked to thousands of nearby nerve cells in an elaborate architecture of branching transmitters called axons and receptors called dendrites.

Yet this mass of matter is in some respects as fragile as it is complex, and time can be its particular enemy. By the age of twenty, the brain is losing mass at the rate of one gram per year. On average, 50,000 neurons die each day, and the overall speed of thought declines apace. At the bitter end, the brain weighs 10 percent less than when it came into the world.

The mental frailties popularly associated with old age—slowed performance, weak memory, reduced creativity—are often blamed on the tendency of the brain to shrink with time. But these problems may not be related to loss of bulk so much as to a degeneration of structure in the nervous system. Each cell's branching dendrites, the fine filaments that gather signals from other cells, seem to die back as they age, like trees whose branches wither in a blighted forest. It is not known whether this occurs because the brain is being asked to process less information or because the channels of communication are becoming physically blocked with debris. But the result is clear: Old brains are less agile and active than young ones.

Yet the postadolescent life of the mind need not be bleak, especially if humans emulate the rats that live—and play—in the laboratory of anatomy professor Marian Cleeves Diamond at the University of California, Berkeley. Diamond built a kind of amusement park for her rodents, consisting of an ever-changing assortment of ladders, wheels, and mazes. This environment, she found, stimulated the rats so vigorously that their brains actually grew new dendrites. Human brains can also grow new dendritic links, according to Diamond.

Rodents of all ages improved. Even the old ones could learn new tricks, although it took them longer. Diamond's research suggests that it may be possible to keep the brain active well into old age by

Still young at heart, octogenarian Danes learn jazz dance from an enthusiastic young instructor, claiming afterward that they felt as if they were in their twenties again.

deliberately challenging it with new mental and physical tasks.

But mental challenge will not heal all. The application of new tasks to the old mind cannot offset the decline of mental speed. Just as with walking and talking, older people need more time than the young to process thoughts. Still, an active, clever mind, even one that operates slowly, may be more adept and entertaining than one of any age that is merely fast. □

New self-awareness tells this twenty-one-month-old that the mirror's image is hers, a concept usually not grasped by children only a few months younger.

Monkey See

When a monkey peers at its own image in the mirror, it perceives nothing very special—just another monkey, according to self-perception researchers. A chimpanzee, on the other hand, seems to recognize itself—not the same way an adult human does but perhaps in the style of an infant.

Evidence for this comes from experiments conducted in 1969 by Tulane University psychologist Gordon G. Gallup. In his tests, chimps and monkeys were given a dab of red dye on the ear, then put in front of a full-length mirror. Noticing something odd, the monkeys reached out to touch the red ears they saw in the mirror. But chimps, once they had become used to the mirror, reacted differ-

ently: They touched their own ears.

In a similar test with human infants, conducted by Michael Lewis and Jeanne Brooks of the Educational Testing Service, mothers unobtrusively smeared rouge on their babies' noses and then put them in front of a mirror. None of the babies under one year old and only one-quarter of those aged fifteen to eighteen months reached to touch their own nose; but three-quarters of those who were twenty-one months to two years old recognized that the nose in the mirror was their own. The results hint that self-awareness grows gradually with age and sophistication—like learning to walk—and does not strike suddenly, as a flash of infant insight. □

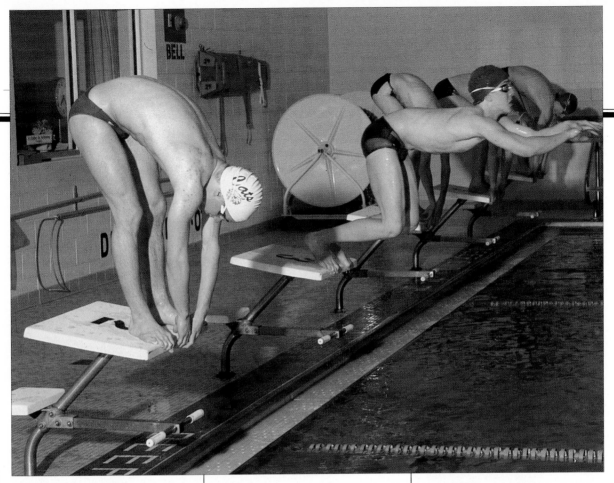

Full of Whoa

A starfish that has been flipped over on its back immediately tries to right itself. At first, all five legs move at once in a frantic effort to recover an upright position. But gradually the flailing stops. Three legs become still while the other two continue working to push the animal back on its stomach. If its nerve center is damaged, however, all five legs will keep thrashing, and eventually the inverted starfish will die. The example points up one of every brain's most important functions: not to stimulate activity but to limit it.

The concept of the mind as an inhibiting force goes back a long way. Aristotle noticed that a person cannot talk and listen to music at the same time. The mind blocks one sensation to focus on another. But it was not until 1884 that British neurologist John Hughlings Jackson laid out a medical theory of control levels in the brain. He saw a parallel with society, comparing the mind to a government that must always be alert for anarchic rebellions among the lower orders—that is, among the limbs. He formed this idea by observing the spastic movements of epileptics, including his wife. The healthy mind, concluded Jackson and many others since, works less by excitation than by inhibition.

Thus, obsessive behavior springs from an inability to shut down an impulse to wash or wring one's hands, and schizophrenics often suffer an unmanageable torrent of confused thoughts. The firing of more than a small fraction of the brain's neurons produces the kind of electrical storm seen in epileptic seizures (*page 19*).

Inhibition-destroying chemicals

The inhibiting action of the mind is not infallible, as here, when a swimmer jumps the gun.

abound. Strychnine, a potent poison that blocks the brain's inhibiting action, throws the victim into violent convulsions. Poisons produced by tetanus (lockjaw) bacteria also erode these inhibitors.

When inhibitions are subverted, one primitive reflex left ungoverned is aggressive behavior. Usually, violent responses are held in check. But researchers have found that these responses can be loosed by electrically stimulating a primitive area deep in the brain called the limbic system (*page 17*). Similarly, aggressive behavior can be released by flooding the brain with a mild poison that liberates the limbic system from the restraints of intelligence: alcohol. □

Playing with Brain

Coaches often teach that success in sports requires not just physical training but mental discipline as well. In recent years, a number of famous athletes have taken the idea a step beyond discipline to use visualization—a kind of rehearsal in the mind—to gain an edge on their competitors. They create mental movies of themselves succeeding at some particular task—such as hitting a golf ball perfectly—and play the pictures over internally. Then they try to transfer the successful image from the mind to the body and beyond, to the world at large.

One famous practitioner of this method is Jack Nicklaus, the champion golfer. "I never hit a shot, even in practice, without having a very sharp, in-focus picture of it in my head," Nicklaus wrote in *Golf My Way*. "First I 'see' the ball where I want it to finish, nice and white and sitting up high on the bright green grass. Then the scene quickly changes and I 'see' the ball going there." Finally, the movie "shows me making the kind of swing that will turn the previous images into reality."

Other athletes who say they have used mental rehearsal as a training discipline are Olympic diver Greg Louganis, Olympic decathlete gold medalist Bruce Jenner, the great football running back O. J. Simpson, and tennis champions Chris Evert and Martina Navratilova. One advantage of such internal practice, the users say, is that it is possible to slow down time and thus perfect each increment of any given action—by spending minutes constructing a perfect high dive, for example, that will actually be executed in a second or two.

These tricks are nothing new to the Russians and East Europeans, according to American weightlifter Charles Garfield. He claims that Olympic athletes from the former Eastern bloc have long been aware of the advantages of visualization and have used it systematically to boost performance. After Soviet trainers showed him how to imprint a successful image in his own mind, Garfield reports, he could bench-press 365 pounds of weights, even though he had done no lifting for months. □

Golf champion Jack Nicklaus chips out of the rough, a successful shot that, like all of this golfer's shots, was first visualized in great detail.

Where There's Hope

One of the mind's most resilient features is its tenacious grasp on hope, and a powerful aversion to its opposite, despair. In the final extremity, hope means life, and it is death for the mind to relinquish it. Nowhere was this demonstrated to more sobering effect than in accounts of captivity in the Nazi death camps of World War II.

Viktor Frankl, who lived to describe his ordeal in a book called *Man's Search for Meaning*, has provided a rare insight into the role of hope and despair in that worst of all possible worlds. As a psychiatrist, he was uniquely qualified to describe the psychic dimensions of his ordeal. He later claimed that he survived largely by keeping hope alive in his thoughts. "Man can preserve a vestige of spiritual freedom, of independence of mind" even in the hellish conditions of Auschwitz, he wrote.

Everything depends on conviction, according to Frankl. His strength of spirit and mind kept him alive. But other people around him slipped into mental despair and from there, inevitably, into death. A sure sign of giving up, Frankl recalled, was to smoke the cigarettes that were given out in the camp as payment for dangerous jobs. Cigarettes could be traded for soup, and anyone who chose the momentary pleasure of smoking over food was doomed. "When we saw a comrade smoking his own cigarettes," he explained, "we knew he had given up faith in his strength to carry on, and, once lost, the will to live seldom returned."

The prisoner who lost faith in the future condemned himself. Yet it was risky to put one's hope in anything too specific, such as a calendar date. The death rate in the camp shot up during the Christmas season of 1944, Frankl reported, because many had told themselves they would be free by the new year. When this hope died, they died. One comrade of Frankl's dreamed that the war would be over by March 30, 1945. This gave him a reason to live, but only temporarily. The news from the front turned bad in March, and suddenly, as it became clear that the expected relief would not come after all, the dreamer fell sick and delirious. He died of typhus on March 31, not six weeks before the German surrender. Frankl concluded: "The sudden loss of hope can have a deadly effect," weakening the body's ability to resist disease.

On the other hand, Frankl noted how the mind sustained some inmates. Sensitive people accustomed to a rich intellectual life appeared to suffer more physically than their duller, hardier companions, but in the end, they seemed less damaged mentally by their experiences. "They were able to retreat from their terrible surroundings," Frankl said, "to a life of inner riches and spiritual freedom." □

Fresh Perspective

"The human mind can't be busy with two things at the same moment," wrote Dutch artist Maurits C. Escher. He took great pleasure in teasing the mind about its habits, drawing scenes that twist reality into visual puzzles. He loved to squeeze two opposite and contradictory meanings into one space, overwhelming the mind with ambiguity and uncertainty.

Shy and withdrawn as a child, Escher built a complex world of his own around the geometric problems involved in reducing three-dimensional reality to the two dimensions of paper. He pursued his obsession for thirty years in poverty, unknown outside of a small graphic arts community in the Netherlands. Escher was not "discovered" until the 1950s; since then his work has been reproduced worldwide. "It is satisfying to note that quite a few people enjoy this kind of playfulness," Escher said, "and that they aren't afraid to modify their thinking about rock-solid realities."

His drawings and etchings—black geese becoming white geese, people climbing stairs that become ceilings—seem both credible and impossible. They are meant to raise disturbing questions. "I can't keep from fooling around with our irrefutable certainties," Escher said on accepting Hilversum's Culture Prize in 1965. He enjoyed mixing up perspectives and turning gravity on its head. "Are you really sure," he asked, "that a floor can't also be a ceiling? Are you definitely convinced that you will be on a higher plane when you walk up a staircase?" □

Whispers

Information seems to come to the conscious mind directly from the outside world. In fact, every scrap filters through a subconscious channel hidden from the waking self. Psychologists have known for more than a century that this subconscious mind influences behavior in mysterious ways—and have sought better access to it. Hypnotism, for example, was invented as a means of entering this hidden corner of the mind.

But researchers have also explored ways to speak to the subconscious mind in a voice the conscious mind cannot hear—in a subliminal voice. In the 1980s, Howard Shevrin, a neuroscientist at the University of Michigan, found evidence not only that such communication is possible but that the brain responds differently to the same message depending on how rapidly the message is conveyed. Using subjects with scalp sensors to detect electric activity, Shevrin flashed the word *fear* on a screen, sometimes very rapidly, sometimes more slowly. He found that the subject's brain responded about twice as quickly when the word was signaled rapidly, suggesting that it was being received only by the subconscious.

Many attempts have been made to use this subconscious channel to send messages to people without their knowing it. Something like panic swept across America in the late 1950s when author Vance Packard reported that some advertising agencies had considered hiring hypnotists to design commercials. Packard's research led to the discovery that one movie theater operator in Fort Lee, New Jersey, had run secret messages on the screen—"DRINK COKE" and "EAT POPCORN"—flashed too rapidly for the conscious mind to notice. The theater manager said sales went up during the intermissions; but he was unable to repeat the alleged result.

Even so, the news triggered a public outcry, and broadcasting industry executives responded by agreeing to ban all such ads from radio and television. However, one ad did slip past the censors. A manufacturer of a family game called Husker Du flashed out a quick, subliminal television message just before Christmas in 1973 saying, "GET IT!" History does not tell whether the children who saw it—or their parents—responded.

Investigating sneaky ads such as this has become a full-time occupation for media analyst Wilson Bryan Key. From Mediaprobe, his center in Reno, Nevada, the media gadfly examines the minutiae of TV and magazine commercials for concealed images. Key has discerned pornography hidden in whiskey bottles and salacious words and gestures on a cake box. But many experts say his findings are entirely the product of his own imagination. Besides, advertisers argue, there is no evidence that hidden images sell products.

Meanwhile, without knowing how or whether such techniques work, many people have begun to use them for self-improvement. In the United States alone, some five million special subliminal message tapes were reportedly sold in 1988. One company in Michigan sells recordings at $14.95 a copy—along with a special signal decoder costing $169.95—that provide restful music at the conscious level while nagging the subconscious mind to get into shape. The prosperity tape, for example, coos to the customer, "I attract success. I attract money. I deserve the good life." Another tape curbs bad budget habits, whispering, "It feels good to spend money carefully." Some tapes purport to improve sex: "I am motivated physically to show my love." And, for duffers, there is the subliminal golf pro, muttering, "I can putt." □

Tone Deft

Humans have an uncanny ability to find the right meaning in another person's tone of voice—regardless of the words or sounds being uttered. The mind is adept at sifting out the emotional truth, even when the spoken text means something different or absolutely nothing.

Two American speech researchers, Delwin Dusenbery and Franklin Knower, demonstrated this in 1939. They asked a group of people to read out the first eleven letters of the alphabet (a-k), giving each one a different emotional stress such as awe, anger, glee, great pain, and so on. They made twenty-two recordings, selected eight, and then asked other groups of students to interpret them. The results were remarkably consistent. More than 75 percent of the time, the listeners were able to identify the emotion correctly. The sound of "determination" came across most clearly; "religious love" and "laughter" were the least understandable. Women were slightly better than men in their interpretations.

The experiment has been repeated many times since then, in many ways. Sometimes actors have been asked to read standard texts, or singers to sing a note with a particular emotion.

Mothers have also been asked to interpret the sounds of a baby crying. Here, too, the listeners were able to extract meaning from inarticulate bawling. American psychiatrist Peter Wolff concluded in 1969 that the infant cry expresses three distinct moods: anger (loud and prolonged), hunger (rhythmic and repetitive), and pain (sudden and long, with breath held before the cry).

In all cases, the results were similar: The right meaning was sensed even when there were no words to guide the interpretation. Apparently, the mind is less interested in what one says than in how one says it. □

The term *self*—with its modern meaning of a permanent, individual identity—did not enter the English language until 1674, according to the *Oxford English Dictionary*. Then, suddenly aware of this *I*, English speakers coined a half-dozen related terms, including *self-sufficient, self-knowledge, self-made, selfish*, and *self-interest*.

Relevant Ratios

Sheer size is not what counts in measuring brainpower; far more important is the proportion of brain weight to body weight. By this standard, dinosaurs were among the least brainy creatures, the largest having only about one-thousandth of one percent of its body weight allocated to its brain. In contrast, dogs come in at 0.85 percent, and humans at 2.5 percent. But, as always in nature, exceptions complicate the rule: The highly intelligent whale has only three-thousandths of one percent of its great weight in brain; spider monkeys are 4.8 percent brains, and bird-brained sparrows, 4.2. □

The Pushover

A person who develops an obsessive taste for whiskey or drugs is often regarded as a moral failure. But, in fact, the mind is a sucker for substances that alter its reality. And there are plenty to go around—thousands of them, ranging from alcohol to opium.

The mind's drug hunger appears to be universal, crossing time, cultures, and geography. Whether it be Australian Aborigines, Xingú Indians, Eskimo, high-altitude Nepalese, upcountry Africans, or citizens of the industrialized West, most cultures use mind-changing drugs and have from prehistoric times. The modern epidemic of heroin addiction, for example, is rooted in the taking of opium, heroin's chemical grandparent, used since the dawn of civilization. It is not known whether the search—in addicts, the desperate, endless search—for drugs is based merely on a wish to feel good or to blot out reality, or is tied to some biological need—for example, to deficiencies of certain chemicals in the brain.

Whatever the source of the urge, drug taking is not restricted to humans. Birds, bees, elephants, koala bears, cattle, and other animals have been known to get drunk on fermented leaves, fruit, or flowers, or even to seek out mind-altering weeds in the pasture. Like humans, drugged animals get dizzy, stagger, and fall. If they persist, they may get so intoxicated that they suffer injuries or die from starvation. But no one calls them immoral.

Is there perhaps some feature common to human and animal minds that causes both to enjoy being intoxicated? Ronald K. Siegel, a member of the psychiatric faculty at the University of California, Los Angeles, thinks that there is. Siegel calls it the fourth drive of the mind, after the other big motivating forces—the desires of hunger, thirst, and sex. The fourth drive is a general appetite for altering the mind. Siegel's evidence for the theory comes from surveying various animal intoxication reports from such disparate places as Africa, Siberia, Southeast

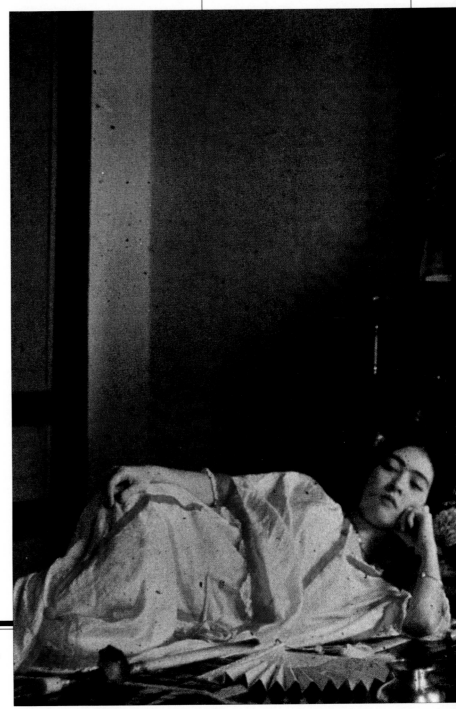

A doomed beauty lounges among a 1915 opium den's paraphernalia of addiction in French Indochina.

Asia, Europe, and North America.

For example, it is well known that cats get high on the herb *Nepeta cataria*, or catnip. They seek it out, first sniffing and chewing, then staring with a blank expression into space. Frequently it caus-es sexual arousal, and some animals are more sensitive to it than others. For example, one young tiger was observed to take a whiff of the herb, leap up several feet, urinate in midair, fall flat on his back, then jump up and dash headlong into the side of his cage.

But there are many more obscure intoxicants, too—such as *iboga* root, the vice of choice for wild boars in the forests of central Africa. After digging up and eating some *iboga*, the boars report- ◊

edly go into wild frenzies, jumping about and displaying fear and flight reactions. An alkaloid was extracted from this plant in the lab that produced hallucinogenic symptoms in dogs. Jane Goodall, famed for her work in the wild with chimpanzees, has reported seeing a wild jackal cub eat a mushroom, after which the animal "seemed to go mad," rushing around in circles, then charging straight at a gazelle and a bull wildebeest.

But as anthropomorphic as such behavior may seem, there *is* a basic difference between animal and human intoxication: degree. Supplies of intoxicants in the wild are limited, occurring generally only once a year when fruit turns ripe. The human mind has devised ways to produce mind-altering substances year-round, in unlimited quantity. Intoxication may be the fourth biological drive; but addiction, an oddity in the natural world, is a self-inflicted human plague. □

Bows, Zen Arrows

The master of Zen archery plucks an arrow, lifts a six-foot bow over his head, and extends the string—all in a single movement that appears to demand no physical effort. The archer seems unaware of the target. Suddenly, as though spontaneously, the arrow leaps from his bow with a loud crack and soars to a black bull's-eye many yards away. Then he prepares a second shot and repeats the feat, sending the second arrow to bisect the first on the distant target.

How is it done? The Zen master would deny that the feat was "done" at all. If asked what held his attention as he prepared to shoot—an act that would seem to require great concentration—he would say, "Nothing." On the contrary, the whole purpose of this incredibly disciplined performance is to show the power of what might be called "unthought." The goal is to empty the head of every thought and deny the conscious self, turning over the interior controls to the "everyday mind" that governs routine behavior—walking, eating, sleeping—and to remain relaxed. In this condition, as the Zen instructor would say, the archer, the bow, and the target become one. The arrow "shoots itself."

Determined to learn the secrets of this art, German philosopher Eugen Herrigel became a pupil, during the 1920s, of one of the great Zen archers in Tokyo, Kenzo Awa. The German's description of the six years he spent learning to use the bow and arrow is a record of Herrigel's self-conscious Western mind struggling against, and finally yielding to, the ego-suppressing Eastern mentality of Awa.

When Herrigel first drew the bow, his hands shook and his breathing was loud and labored. In time, he learned to control his breathing so it was as smooth as the master's; his muscles grew calm. Learning to release the string and hit the target were harder tasks. Herrigel became frustrated when he could not hold the bow long enough and steadily enough to achieve a graceful release. "You haven't really let go of yourself," the master scolded. The shot should "fall" from the bow, he said, just as snow falls effortlessly from a bamboo leaf. After detaching himself further from the physical effort and practicing many more months, Herrigel began to succeed. "How it happened," he wrote, "I could not explain then and I cannot explain today."

But there may be a plausible scientific explanation. Zen training may succeed because it gives control of the body directly to the part of the mind that smoothly coordinates muscle movement. This area, located at the lower back part of the brain, is called the cerebellum. Operating below the level of consciousness, the cerebellum appears to contain programs for moving many parts of the body in coordination. Damage to the cerebellum results in jerky, poorly regulated motions: For example, a simple attempt to touch the tip of the nose might accidentally trigger a punch in the face.

It may be that when a person "chokes" in performing some well-practiced skill—hitting a baseball, for example—signals from the cerebellum have been interrupted. Too much thinking may be to blame. The goal of Zen training is to banish these moments of hesitation by suppressing conscious thought. By keeping the self entirely out of mind, it may be possible to open a free-flowing channel between the unconscious mind and the muscles that it controls—to let the arrow, whatever the arrow may be, shoot itself. □

A Japanese archer prepares to draw a long bow, once used by horse-mounted warriors and now part of *kyudo,* "the way of the bow," a physical and spiritual discipline based on mental tranquillity.

Back to Basics

Love may be the noblest human sentiment, but if theories of emotional evolution are right, it appeared first not in human suitors but in cousins of the rat, the mole, and the shrew. The ancestors of these little creatures were probably the first to have any emotions at all, the most important of which was love—parental, not romantic.

Humans have inherited the early mammals' instincts for parenthood, according to brain researcher Paul D. MacLean of the National Institute of Mental Health in Poolesville, Maryland. He believes people have what he calls a triune brain—three distinct but interconnected brains, each with different behavioral instincts, encapsulated in a single human mind. Within every human being, MacLean says, are a reptile brain, an old mammal brain, and a neocortex—the highly developed outermost and newest layer of the cerebral cortex.

The reptile brain developed about 300 million years ago. It lies deep within the skull, just above where the spinal cord enters the head. MacLean calls this the R-complex. Next came the limbic system, an area that surrounds the R-complex and that developed about 200 million years ago. Although present in rep-

tiles in a rudimentary form, it is mainly associated with early mammals. Surrounding these two on the outside is the neocortex, or "new mammal brain," the most human part, which first arose 60 million or more years ago.

The reptile brain, according to MacLean, regulates the struggle for power, daily routines, imitation, and deception. The old mammal brain is concerned with nursing, vocal communication between parents and offspring, and play. And the neocortex, the most complex area, humans use to solve problems, plan for the future, and control speaking and writing.

The intermeshing triple signals of the triune brain are much more sophisticated in humans than in animals.

Even so, MacLean finds fascinating parallels between some human and animal patterns of behavior.

The territorial obsessions of West Africa's beautiful rainbow lizard offer a case in point. A young male must show politeness by bowing his head whenever he meets a senior male or when the ruling lizard performs an assertive display. This "signature" typically consists of a push-up followed by several nods of the head. Failure to defer to elders will lead to a fight, one that the young lizard is likely to lose. As they mature, males who are to have offspring must leave home and establish a new territory of their own. If a stranger approaches the territory of another male, a confrontation ensues.

When this happens, the home lizard tries to scare off the

Neomammalian

Paleomammalian
(Limbic System)

Reptilian

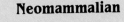

The human brain, according to researcher Paul D. MacLean, is really three brains: a central one like the reptiles', overlaid by another that resembles early mammals', within a layer unique to primates.

intruder with visible threats, puffing himself up and raising his back spines. If this deterrent fails, the defender rushes down and squares off for a tail-swinging battle. MacLean tells of one harried home lizard dashing about a woodpile like a "frenzied manager," trying to mate with two females while rushing every so often to the top of the pile to warn off an intruder. Over a period of weeks, he gradually lost control of the territory, and the interloper began mating with the females. Now and then, the brazen outsider would even climb to the top of the woodpile and give his own signature display.

Similar territorial imperatives, MacLean argues, are seen in wild cats and dogs, which mark their territory with scent and defend it against intruders. Even gorillas engage in confrontational standoffs between resident and intruding males that evoke the rainbow lizard's fights.

To MacLean, such behavior is evident in many aspects of human life as well, suggesting that the polite nod, bow, or handshake traces back to our reptilian instincts. As for boundary markers, he sees them everywhere: in graffiti, stone monuments, town walls, and even guest books. All of them, he says, may be hand-me-downs from the old, reptilian way of life.

Fortunately, the inner reptile is encased in a sweeter disposition and rarely has the final say. Thus, while a lizard, having reproduced, is as likely as not to eat its hatchlings, mammals tend to nurture, not devour, their young. In the triune brain, love conquers all. □

Ghosts

Medical records reaching back more than 400 years show that people who lose an arm, a leg, or another body part say they still detect feelings in the missing appendage. They often describe a tingling, a sharp pang, or sensations of squeezing or abnormal heat—pains where, reason says, nothing exists that could hurt.

For some victims, the impression is extremely vivid. One report tells of a sailor who accidentally severed his right index finger. For forty years, he could not escape the feeling that the finger was still there—no longer flexible, but rigidly extended. Every time he lifted a spoon to his mouth or rubbed his face, he cringed away from the phantom digit, although he knew intellectually that it was not really there. In another case, surgeons removed the arm of a cancer patient, and the ghost limb that replaced it became a severe annoyance. The patient could not suppress the feeling that the missing arm was in constant motion. Its flailings kept her from sleeping, and she told people to stay away from her left side because she did not want to hit them.

Despite centuries of such testimony, some physicians have dismissed phantom limb complaints as fantasies or worse—as signs of mental illness. But doctors who specialize in treating amputees believe nearly all patients have these sensations, at least for a time. The experts disagree, however, on whether it is normal to feel pain in the missing limb. Some

say pain occurs in no more than 5 percent of amputees. Others report that up to 90 percent occasionally suffer phantom distress.

Three theories have been proposed to explain why these sensations might persist after the nerves have been severed. One is that emotional stress causes the amputee to create a fantasy limb to make up for the loss. A second idea is that irritants such as scar tissue at the stump of the lost limb may trigger the phantom sensation. The third—which has gradually won acceptance—is that the feelings are genuine and originate in the mind itself.

If the last idea is correct, it means every person carries a map of the entire body in his or her mind. The right leg, for example, exists in two places: in the physical limb attached to the hip and in an abstract form in the head. These two perceptions are coupled in childhood, becoming a single representation. But if the physical limb is removed, its mental counterpart may live on. From time to time, nerve cells in the brain may "leak" signals to adjacent cells that represent the missing leg and stimulate them indirectly, bringing the phantom to life.

Some experts think ghost images such as these are present in the mind from birth. Evidence for this can be found in research done at the Albert Einstein College of Medicine in New York, involving children born missing a limb. Of 101 children examined, 18 said they had experienced sensations from a limb they had never possessed—a phantom limb indeed. □

A Perfect Spy

The conscious mind is the mental surface on which the senses lay their perceptions—the sights, smells, and sounds that people use to comprehend their complex world. But researchers are now detecting evidence of another, deeper sensory apparatus: If the conscious mind is somehow impaired, it seems, a secret array of senses in the unconscious may go to work. Thus, blind people may sometimes "see" a flash of light, brought to them, some scientists believe, along little-used, vestigial pathways in the brain. Some brain-damage victims use implements they can no longer identify or experience leaps of the heart at the sight of a loved one whose identity is forever lost to them. Apparently, the unconscious is able to provide a crude substitute for some types of lost memory or sensation.

Called covert awareness, this inner spy was first suggested by a Swiss psychologist nearly a century ago but did not seem to be an important aspect of the mind's operation until the 1970s. Then, researchers began to use a technique called forced-choice guessing to study how memory operates.

For example, subjects are given a complex piece of information to remember but cannot recall it moments later. However, when asked to select that information from several similar pieces, they almost invariably pick the one they had been unable to memorize. Results of such tests suggest that a clandestine mental operative sees and remembers when the conscious mind does not.

Now used to describe a host of variations on the theme of unconscious senses, covert awareness does more than help out when other senses fail—it also reinforces existing mental functions, especially the way humans make decisions. Conversely, when contact with this secret inner eye and ear is lost, human decision-making processes may take a turn for the bizarre. Patients with certain types of brain damage, for example, may replace a steady, happy Dr. Jekyll with an aberrantly behaving, anti-social Mr. Hyde. The stricken individual can no longer make good decisions, researchers believe, because he or she has been cut off from one of the mind's least-understood, but most familiar, forms of covert awareness: the gut feeling, the hunch. □

THE MIND AT WORK

The mind is an engine of intelligence and intuition, propelled by a largely secret life within. Assessing its performance is difficult, not because there are no measurable elements, but because there are so many. If one conceives of intelligence as the horsepower of the mind, which expresses itself in language, a rough idea emerges of what the mind is able to do.

But mental performance is not fixed by rules of intellectual engineering. Some minds are so powerful that all kinds of knowledge are easily assimilated and wisdom arrives without the benefit of years. Some transmit on only a single channel, counting or memorizing or executing art, but unable, or unwilling, to speak. Some perfectly able minds live, incredibly, in the merest crust of brain tissue. Although it does not always employ the same tools or tongues, the human mind is a determined machine, powerfully impelled to comprehend its world.

Bent Twig

For William James Sidis, a fine mind—perhaps one of history's best—became a kind of deformity. Instead of following the expected meteoric career, the child prodigy opted for what seemed a life of mediocre obscurity that earned him the hatred of a disappointed public and press.

Born in 1898 and named for his father's mentor and colleague, psychologist-philosopher William James, Sidis began his rise to fame at the age of four, when he could use a typewriter to produce both English and French. By five, he could speak five languages and read Plato in the original Greek. Learning a new language was the work of a day for the young genius.

The impetus for this extraordinary development was his father, Boris Sidis, a Russian-born psychiatrist then teaching at Harvard. The elder Sidis was convinced that geniuses are made the way twigs are bent, and he showed off his son to the world as proof of his theory. But young Sidis's mind was naturally spectacular: One psychometrician later estimated his IQ at between 250 and 300.

Under his father's unrelenting tutelage and the glare of publicity (stories about him would appear on the first page of the *New York Times* nineteen times), Sidis finished his first year of high school and applied for admission to Harvard at the age of nine. Although he passed the entrance examinations, he was rejected on the ground that he was too immature emotionally for college life. Admitted as Harvard's youngest scholar when he was eleven, he amazed his elders with a lecture on the fourth dimension that was beyond the grasp of many professors.

Brilliant as he was, however, Sidis appeared to be out of his depth at Harvard socially and emotionally. Many of his classmates regarded him as eccentric and reclusive. Sidis nevertheless graduated cum laude in 1914, at sixteen. "I want to live the perfect life," he told reporters at the time. "The only way to live the perfect life is to live it in seclusion." His remarks were prophetic.

He taught briefly at Houston's Rice Institute, then entered Harvard Law School. Increasingly radical politically, he left school in 1918, just before graduating. Then, as a conscientious objector and a budding Marxist, he was arrested during a May Day riot in Boston and narrowly saved from jail by his parents. But the incident apparent-

William James Sidis, shown at left at age eight, possessed what may have been one of the greatest minds of all time. He was, at eleven, the youngest scholar ever admitted to Harvard. In later life he became, among other things, a preeminent *peridromophile* —his term for serious collectors of streetcar transfers *(above)*.

ly jarred him, for from then on, he seemed to drop out of the intellectual race he had run all his life.

Sidis took a series of undemanding jobs, apparently discarding all challenging pursuits. He did write one book about a hobby that became a passion: *Notes on the Collection of Streetcar Transfers*. He even coined a word for such collectors, *peridromophiles.*

The press took to attacking the one-time boy wonder as a burnout who had been too smart too soon. A James Thurber article in the *New Yorker* in 1937 ridiculed him so savagely that Sidis sued for libel, finally winning a small out-of-court settlement. Editorials ac-

cused him of betraying the public's expectations. But, although Sidis went his own way, he never really abandoned the inner life of the mind. Instead, as one writer put it, Sidis merely took his intelligence underground.

Three decades after Sidis's death in 1944 of a brain hemorrhage, a Columbia University psychology student by the name of Dan Mahony began probing the lost years of Sidis's life. After much rummaging in dusty attics, Mahony found that Sidis had in fact filled those seemingly empty years with mental activity. He had many friends, whom he amazed with such feats as doing a *New York Times* crossword puzzle entirely from memory after quickly reading the clues. He could translate some forty languages, and he wrote prodigiously. There were manuscripts for two books and evidence of two more, as well as eighty-nine newspaper columns written under a pen name. His sister, Helena, thought that there must be a dozen more manuscripts, including one book about the lost continent of At-

lantis and a science fiction novel.

One of the surviving books, *The Animate and the Inanimate*, published in 1925, put forward a number of precocious theories of the universe, including a description of the cosmic phenomena now called black holes—collapsed stars so dense that their powerful gravity prevents even the escape of light.

Another book, a 1,200-page tome called *The Tribes and the States*, argued from persuasive evidence that the political system of New England was profoundly influenced by the democratic federation of its Indian tribes. Sidis's search for seclusion, some scholars now believe, came from his having adopted the teachings of the Okamakammessetts, a Massachusetts tribe that taught a principle of anonymous contribution to society.

But the legacy of the man once called "the most remarkable youth in the world" was a general sense that neurotic failure was the inescapable fate of child prodigies. In fact, by jeering at his differences, the world had silenced one of its finest minds. □

Quick Study

Child prodigies are widely believed to fall back to more average abilities as they grow older, in keeping with the folk axiom "Early ripe, early rot." But for some, such as little Christian Heineken, there is barely time for the precocious mind to ripen, much less to fail.

Christian was born in Lübeck, Germany, in 1721, the son of a painter. As his mother could not nurse him, the parents hired Sophie Hildebrand, a soldier's wife, as a wet nurse—and Christian's lifelong companion. When the child began talking at the age of ten months, the Heinekens hired a tutor to nurture Christian's clearly prodigious mind. Under the guidance of Christian von Schoeneich, the boy learned to recount the major stories in the five books of Moses before his first birthday; by fourteen months, he had learned the rest of the Bible.

Von Schoeneich then moved on to history, and by two and a half Christian was familiar with the wars and empires of the Hebrews, Egyptians, Assyrians, Phoenicians, Persians, Greeks, and Romans. He had also mastered the geography of contemporary Europe—its countries, cities, seas, and rivers. None of it was merely rote learning. Although Christian seemed to remember virtually everything he was told, he always fit information into an appropriate context.

At two and a half, the previously healthy lad was struck by the first in a series of debilitating illnesses. Returning to his studies several months later, Christian spent a productive interval studying Roman law (in Latin) and Danish history. By the time he was four, he was well versed in European history.

Another bout of sickness led his parents to suggest that a little trip might be beneficial. Allowed to pick the destination, Christian chose Copenhagen. He wanted to present a set of painted maps to King Frederick IV of Denmark. This was hardly an unreasonable request for a boy famous throughout half of Europe, and the trip was soon arranged. In July of 1724, Christian, his parents, and Sophie, still his main source of nourishment, set out to see the king.

The royal audience was postponed once because of Christian's poor health, but by September he had recovered enough to dazzle the king and his court—and to worry them with his obvious frailty.

Not long after his return to Lübeck in October, Christian fell ill again. He slipped into and out of a coma for almost nine weeks. In moments of partial improvement, he began the study of astronomy, but this time, there would be no recovery. Christian Heineken died in June 1725, aged four years, four months, and twenty-one days, utterly worn out. □

A copy of a 1726 etching that may have been presented to Denmark's King Frederick shows the German prodigy Christian Henrich Heineken among symbols of great learning.

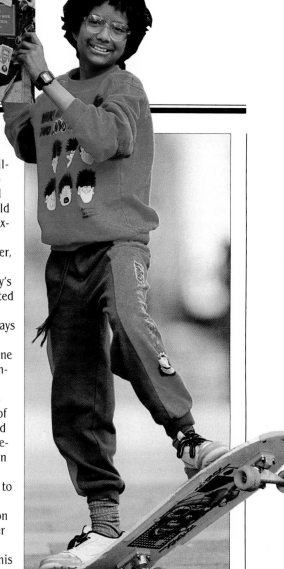

In 1990, eleven-year-old Ganesh Sittampalam *(right)* became the youngest person admitted to a British university since the Middle Ages.

Bloomers

In a kind of sweepstakes of the mind, an eleven-year-old boy from southwest London in 1990 became the youngest person to be admitted to a British university since the Middle Ages. Enrolled at the University of Surrey just seven months after his eleventh birthday, Ganesh Sittampalam edged out the previous record holder, Ruth Lawrence, who eight years earlier had entered Oxford University at the age of twelve years two months.

Although both youngsters display superb equipment for tackling advanced mathematics, they came to celebrity by very different paths. When Ruth Lawrence was five, her father, Harry, quit his job as a computer consultant to devote himself to her education. All the teaching took place in the Lawrence family kitchen in Huddersfield, Yorkshire. Ruth never attended ordinary classes until she began undergraduate work in mathematics at Oxford.

When Ruth left for Oxford on a scholarship in 1982, her father went with her. Pedaling about the campus and town on a tandem bicycle, Harry accompanied his daughter to every lecture, meal, and tutorial. She finished her work for a math degree in two years, then completed a physics degree in her third year. Moving on to graduate work, Ruth took a teaching position at her Oxford college when she was fifteen. She received a math doctorate in 1989, becoming, at eighteen, the youngest scholar ever to take an advanced degree in Britain. When Ruth took up a fellowship at Harvard, Harry Lawrence went to America with her.

In contrast, Ganesh Sittampalam has been made to follow a normal course of education, with other, more ordinary children. "We did not want to go down the Ruth Lawrence road because we thought that would be a worrying thing to do," explained Arjuna Sittampalam, Ganesh's physics-trained father, who is now a London investment banker. Instead, the boy's parents have kept their talented son in King's College Junior School in Wimbledon. Four days a week, he wears his school's red blazer to classes there. One day each week, he dons a Dennis the Menace track suit to join students nearly twice his age at the nearby University of Surrey, where he was admitted to the second year of a mathematics course after earning an *A* on the first-year math test.

Curiously, Ganesh planned to wait until 1992 to take the common entrance examination before determining his further education plans. By then, he would probably already have his bachelor's degree. □

Lost Art

Prodigious calculating skills sometimes vanish as mysteriously as they appear. While trauma may be the cause of some losses—one nine-year-old lost his extraordinary arithmetic ability within weeks of his father's death—disuse is probably the more common reason.

One case in point was Zerah Colburn, a famous nineteenth-century prodigy who needed just five seconds to find the cube root of 413,993,348,677, could instantly factor six-digit numbers, and raised numbers to their sixteenth power with ease. Exhibited before admiring crowds by his ambitious father, Colburn honed his calculating ability to a high level. But when he was sent to school, attention to other subjects apparently displaced it; by the time he was twenty, he was merely an ordinary arithmetician. Apparently his mind, like that of a linguist, needed exercise to maintain its fluency. □

The Calculating Boy

As wondrous as the feats of lightning calculators appear to most people, they are in fact based on techniques that almost anyone can understand—if not replicate. Among the best-known methods are those of George Parker Bidder, a child prodigy who toured Britain in the early nineteenth century, demonstrating his talents.

Bidder was born in 1806, the son of a Devonshire stonemason. Often truant from the school he entered at age six, he learned counting from his older brother, also a mason. Without knowing the written numerals that represented numbers, Bidder quickly learned to count to 10, then to 100.

Fascinated by his new skill, Bidder began to play with the numbers. He found that he could get to 100 much faster by counting to ten, stopping and repeating: Two times made twenty, three times made thirty, and so on. Bidder later claimed that this simple process helped him gain complete familiarity with all the numbers up to 100. "They became as it were my friends, and I knew all their relations and acquaintances."

Then, without knowing what the word *multiply* meant, he taught himself multiplication by arranging peas or marbles in rectangles of rows and columns, then counting them. Thus, working alone, Bidder evolved his own understanding of numbers and even his own algebra before he learned to read or write; indeed, he later doubted that he could have acquired his powerful calculating ability in a conventional classroom.

One day, playing in the shop of a blacksmith, he called out the answer to an overheard arithmetic problem. The astonished workers put more questions to the lad, who answered all correctly. Learning that he could earn small change for such tricks, Bidder began to cultivate his skills, of which multiplication was the most advanced. Soon he was good enough that his father, too, saw the financial potential and took the boy out of school to exhibit him for profit.

The Calculating Boy was not quite nine when he was presented to the queen and answered several difficult questions. One posed by the royal astronomer, Sir William Herschel, was typical: "Light travels from the Sun to the Earth in eight minutes, the Sun being 98 million miles off. If light would take six years and four months traveling at the same rate from the nearest fixed star, how far is that star from Earth?" Bidder took just one minute to arrive at the answer: 40,633,740,000,000 miles.

In performing such calculations, Bidder used not only arithmetical shortcuts, but also his exceptional memory. He could immediately recall how many "barleycorns [thirds of an inch], inches, feet, or yards there were in a league, mile, or furlong," or how many minutes in a year—a bit of knowledge he used in answering Herschel's question.

Bidder also discovered that he could rely on the habits of his audiences: If he was asked for the cube root of a large number, for example, he could assume that the questioner had come to the number by simply cubing some smaller whole number. He could thus limit the range of possible answers by ignoring fractions; his intimate knowledge of whole numbers took care of the rest.

His fame won Bidder the support of wealthy patrons, who helped the stonemason's son go on to study engineering. He won renown, and considerable wealth, as one of the leading civil engineers of his day. He capped his career with the successful construction of the Victoria Docks in Thames marshes near London—a feat that critics had proclaimed impossible.

But, unlike many prodigies, Bidder never lost his interest in mental calculation. At age seventy-two, he amazed a friend by instantaneously working out a complex problem involving the speed and wavelengths of red light. He died two days later. Writing in praise of Bidder's phenomenal mind, a friend said, "To me it was incomprehensible, as difficult to believe as a miracle." □

George Parker Bidder is shown at left at about age thirteen in an unsigned painting said to be by Sir George Hayter.

Wise Guy

No other twentieth-century mind so epitomizes high intelligence as that of Albert Einstein *(below)*, the little professor whose theories largely reconstructed the human view of how the universe works. His public personality was that of the quintessential absent-minded genius, a rumpled man who liked to sail and play the violin between strokes of brilliance. But Einstein was in fact an eminently practical scholar with rare analytical skills.

Despite his willingness to take on daunting questions about the universe, Einstein claimed a child-like sense of wonder about the world. He confronted concepts of time and space with the same awe and pleasure he had experienced as a child contemplating the mysterious movement of the needle on a compass. But however curious and observant he was as a child, he was also hampered by a poor memory and an inclination to cut classes. He rarely did well in school.

Einstein maintained that language had little to do with his thought processes, which were based instead on clear visual images. For example, the theory of relativity, which showed how measurements are affected by motion and gravity, began with Einstein imagining, as a sixteen-year-old, what it would be like to ride a beam of light. ''Imagination,'' he said, ''is more important than knowledge.''

Still, his theory did not appear full-blown in a flash of adolescent genius. Einstein published his first paper on relativity ten years later, while working as a clerk in the Swiss patent office. The complete theory took another decade of intense reflection and refinement, along with his special talent for cutting through inessential details to fundamental principles.

A mind as powerful as Einstein's would seem to demand a special kind of brain to contain it. But his was no larger than average and had no obvious distinguishing features. Some years after his death, however, examination of tissue cut from Einstein's brain suggested an unusual ratio of one kind of brain cell to another. Researchers found that his brain seemed to possess a higher than normal proportion of glial cells, which nourish and support neurons, the fundamental cells of nervous system tissue. Glial cells are known to multiply faster with learning—perhaps leaving in their wake the faint track of a great intelligence. □

Radio Waifs

In the 1940s, the Quiz Kids personified youthful brilliance for Americans. These children, some as young as four, appeared on a nationwide radio show, answering questions about nuclear physics and Wagnerian opera that baffled most of their adult listeners. Professors, businessmen, and senators found themselves stumped in question-and-answer contests with the sharp youngsters.

They were a smash hit, symbols of hope for the future in a decade when the United States emerged from the Great Depression, fought a world war, and saw victory transformed into the nuclear stalemate of the Cold War. The Quiz Kids toured the country, selling war bonds, entertaining troops, and making headlines; they were featured in cartoons and books of paper dolls.

Bright but not bookworms, the Kids looked like the boys and girls next door, putting to rest some of the popular conception that children with good minds must also be eccentric. By glamorizing knowledge, they helped some youngsters discover the pleasures of learning. But not everybody liked them. One adolescent voiced his hope that the Quiz Kids "all turned out to be garbage collectors." Some detractors suspected the group of cheating; one of the Kids was accused of being a midget posing as a little girl.

Nevertheless, the clever Kids seem not to have been greatly troubled by their critics. Instead, they grew up and went on to lives marked by reasonable success. Like most mentally gifted children, they

The 1941 Quiz Kids—from left, Van Dyke Tiers, Lois Karpf, Gerard Darrow, Joan Bishop, and Claude Brenner—stand by to outsmart any adult challengers on the popular national radio show.

arrived at middle age generally healthier, smarter, better educated, and more successful than their contemporaries.

Ruth Duskin Feldman, who became a Quiz Kid in 1941 at seven and stayed with the series until 1950, undertook a retrospective study of the group three decades after the show went off the air in 1953. Contacting 85 of some 600 Kids who appeared on the show, she found that nearly all were college graduates, one-third with doctoral degrees. They were typically employed as lawyers, scientists, professors, executives, and consultants; several had continued in entertainment as actors, producers, and musicians.

Despite their solid success, the grown Quiz Kids included no billionaires, no famous artists, and only one scientifically brilliant standout: James D. Watson, who won the 1962 Nobel Prize in medicine after codiscovering the structure of DNA, the cell's genetic blueprint—work he did before he turned twenty-five. Watson had not been an outstanding Quiz Kid, however, and his specialty then was current events; he took up science only when he got to high school.

For many of the Quiz Kids, their fishbowl celebrity existence was only temporarily troubling. But for at least one, early fame became an insupportable burden. Interviewed anonymously at thirty-nine, a charter Quiz Kid recalled being proclaimed a prodigy at seven and so "obnoxious" at eleven that he was retired from the show five years early. On the whole, however, this early bloomer was pleased with his escape from the program and with the quiet and privacy of his undemanding job: tending roses. □

Smart Alex

To Alexander Craig Aitken *(above)*, extraordinary calculating ability was not just hard to explain; it was impossible to understand. A New Zealander who became an eminent mathematician in Scotland, he never quite comprehended the processes he used to give lightning answers to complex questions.

Aitken found mathematics boring until a high-school algebra teacher piqued his interest by teaching him a trick for calculating the squares of numbers. Captivated, Aitken went straight home to try out similar techniques. So began four years of what he later described as "mental yoga," assiduous practice that honed his skills to a fine edge.

After finishing a higher education interrupted by World War I (he was badly wounded as an infantryman in France), Aitken worked as a teacher at his old high school, then won a scholarship to Edinburgh University in 1923. There, at the age of twenty-eight, he met his first real mathematician; within two years, he earned a doctorate with a highly regarded thesis.

Aitken's computational skills were useful in higher mathematics, but it was mathematics itself, the interactions of quantities and equations, that interested him most. In a fruitful forty-year career, he published eighty papers and several books on mathematics. Nevertheless, his reputation as a calculator continued; in 1954, he delivered a lecture on the subject to the Society of Engineers.

As part of the presentation, Aitken calculated squares (three-digit numbers almost instantaneously, four-digit numbers in about five seconds) and then square roots of some of the same numbers (in two or three seconds). But he could not say how he arrived at his answers; although he was conscious of the stream of calculating activity, he could not describe its details at all. In fact, sometimes the answer came to him so quickly that he could not even tell whether he had calculated it or recalled it from his voluminous memory.

That memory allowed him to store the value of pi to 707 decimal places. "It would have been a reprehensibly useless feat," he said, "had it not been so easy." □

6341082426
× 38254319074
─────────────
24257379039973993524

Dutch Soup

Antoon Van den Hurk *(right)*, a Dutch farmer from Helenaveen, was in his twenties when he heard a radio show called "The Calculating Genius" that featured amazing feats of mental arithmetic. To his surprise, he discovered that he could work out the answers just as fast, without practicing. His mind was a prodigiously powerful natural calculator. During the 1950s, Van den Hurk became famous when journalists wrote about his odd facility with numbers. He even parlayed the skill into a combined theater act with a hypnotist.

The Dutch calculator once explained how he multiplied large numbers, using 6,341,082,426 times 38,254,319,074 as an example. "You just multiply 6,341,082,426 by 38,000,000,000 and remember that solution. Then you multiply 6,341,082,426 by 254,000,000, by 319,000, and by 74. Add them up in your head and you have the answer."

His talent brought him little money, however, and eventually he settled down to work as a laboratory assistant. "One moment one is successful and the next you're forgotten," he told an interviewer in 1982. "That's how life works." □

Roots

Shakuntala Devi makes her living with a mind that outpaces some computers. The diminutive, sari-clad woman is a lightning calculator, performing enormous arithmetic feats in just seconds or faultlessly naming the day of the week for any date in the distant past or future.

A native of Bangalore, India, Devi has been displaying her mental abilities since her poverty-stricken childhood. Her aging father took her from town to town, having Devi stand atop a table to give audiences a glimpse of the tiny prodigy. When her father was too old to continue, Devi pushed on without him, sending most of her earnings home.

As an adult, Devi traded her tabletops for stages around the world. One of her typical feats dur-

Clad in a shimmering blue-and-green sari, diminutive Bangalore calculator Shakuntala Devi solves intricate mathematical problems at lightning speed at a 1976 gathering of State Bank of India employees in New York.

ing performances involves adding four nine-digit numbers, then multiplying the sum by a four-digit number, all within twenty seconds. The *Guinness Book of World Records* lists her correct multiplication of two thirteen-digit numbers, accomplished in twenty-eight seconds. Asked for the twenty-third root of a 201-digit number, she produced an answer in fifty seconds: 546,372,891, the number that a large computer had taken more than a minute to raise to its 201-digit twenty-third power.

Her mind appears to operate as an idiosyncratic computer, using shortcuts called algorithms to bridge large numbers. "I have to start with the simple problems first," she has said, meaning the cube root of a five-digit number. "I have to be relaxed. I try to clear my mind. I don't watch TV on the day I perform; I don't get into conversations. I can work about ninety minutes, and then I get tired."

But Devi is not equally quick with all dates and numbers. She has occasionally come up with the wrong answer and has difficulty remembering her date of birth, which has been variously reported as 1920, 1932, and 1940. And in London, after miscalculating her baby's 1971 due date, she bore the child during a stop at London's Heathrow Airport. □

Grooving

Among the mind's myriad abilities are some that seem, on the surface at least, to have nothing to do with intellect. One of these is the unique talent of Dr. Arthur Lintgen *(below)*, a Philadelphia physician whose perception is so acute that he once recognized Beethoven's Fifth Symphony from across a room—by looking at the grooves in a phonograph record that was not playing at the time. "I don't know how I do it," he deadpanned. "I have terrible eyesight."

A music lover, Lintgen discovered his ability to read record grooves at a party in 1978, when, challenged by a friend, he identified music by looking at unlabeled records. News of his odd faculty spread, and within a few years he was featured in articles and on a television show. In the wake of his growing notoriety, he was tested by skeptics, who ultimately decided he was on the up and up. The trick, it turned out, was not a trick at all.

Any keen observer can see the tiny variations in spacing and contour of record grooves and detect the subtle differences in the way they reflect light. Grooves for soft musical passages, for example, look black, while loud passages are silvery; percussive accents create a jagged, sawtooth effect. For the pattern to be recognizable, however, the readings of the grooves must be played back through a mind that, like Lintgen's, is already full of music. □

The Chess Mind

Chess is one of the great exercises the mind has devised to test its ability to concentrate, remember, and invent. The game demands a specific kind of intelligence, able to size up a position rapidly, compare it with similar situations in past games, and choose the right course of action from myriad possibilities.

Throughout most of the long history of the game, the detailed workings of a highly skilled chess mind have remained largely inac-

cessible to nonmasters. Then, in 1985, a new kind of world champion began to illuminate the mental processes behind his daring style.

At the age of twenty-two, Gary Kasparov became the youngest world champion by winning the title from his fellow Soviet Anatoly Karpov with slashing offensive play that overwhelmed Karpov's cautious, defensive style. In the wake of his victory, Kasparov has tried to popularize the game by distilling its abstract essence for people without the chess master's insights.

Chess is much more than general rules about position and relative

strength, Kasparov teaches. The true art is to evaluate and control many disparate factors, such as the number and kinds of pieces on the board, the tactical strengths of their positions, and the amount of time an attack will take to develop. It is, Kasparov maintains, "like controlling chaos."

Kasparov's own brilliant play shows his talent for moving beyond the countless variations in his extraordinary memory. And his greatest moves, in the end, are beyond explanation. "Some positions are so complex that you cannot calculate even two moves ahead," the master has said. "You must use

your intuition. Sometimes I play by my hand, by my smell. That is a great moment, because you have done something completely outrageous."

His intuitive gift served Kasparov well in a 1989 match with a completely different sort of player *(left): Deep Thought,* a computer that had achieved a high international ranking by defeating several grand masters. The machine might well have been named Fast Thought: It could scan 720,000 moves per second. For all its speed, though, the computer could not match the champion's ability to see, as chess players put it, deeply into the board. Kasparov won a resounding victory in two short, lopsided games. □

Land of the Rising Sums

When IQ scores going back more than half a century are used to compare national performance, the results suggest that some cultures hone the mind to a keener edge than others. Japanese students, in particular, consistently do better on IQ tests than their counterparts in other countries. At least 10 percent of the Japanese born in the 1960s have an IQ over 130, compared to fewer than three percent in the United States and Britain. The Japanese also have the highest average IQ in the world: 115.

Most experts attribute such discrepancies not to inherent mental differences, but rather to dissimilar educational approaches. The Japanese not only have the longest school calendar in the industrial world—243 days per year for the average eighth grader, compared to 180 days for an American student—but also devote more time to education in the home, where mothers typically teach letters and numbers to their preschool children. The national zeal for education piles homework even on grade-schoolers, who are said to find it more fun than drudgery.

By challenging young minds, the Japanese educational system produces more than high IQ scores: The nation's elementary and secondary schools rank among the best in the world in mathematics and science. In some areas, though, Japan lags behind other parts of the world.

In language study, Germany and the Soviet Union lead all other countries. Every German student has to study four to eight years of English. Soviet students get early exposure to a second language

At one of more than 20,000 *juku,* or cram schools, in Japan, a determined student wears a headband bearing the motto "Struggle to pass."

from the requirement that all learn Russian, even though school may be taught in one of the USSR's forty-two different indigenous tongues. Devoted to the purity of their own tongue, the French rank first in native-language studies.

Despite the disparity in student skills, however, Western intelligence does not appear to be declining. For five decades, tests in Britain and the United States, as well as Japan, have shown steadily rising average IQs. The increase is probably caused by many factors,

among them improved health and nutrition and greater stimulation from books and educational toys. Smaller families and more leisure for parents may also have contributed to increasing IQs by allowing parents more time for stimulating interaction with their children.

The three-country tests have once again pointed up an apparent gap between West and East—IQ rises of 1.7 points per decade in Britain and 3 points per decade in the United States, against 7.7 points per decade in Japan. □

Horsepower

The quality of the mind called intelligence defies close definition. It obviously relates to the capacity for learning, understanding, and reasoning, but just what it is and what causes it to vary in strength from one mind to another, no one knows. Because intelligence clearly exists, however, scientists have long wished to find a way to measure it. Pursuing the mental equivalent of horsepower and voltage, scientists have developed a broad range of standardized tests to assess intellectual achievement and potential—with mixed results.

The first standardized intelligence test was developed in 1905 by French psychologist Alfred Binet and was intended to help identify children who needed remedial education. It was adapted and expanded in the United States by Lewis Terman of Stanford University, who had bigger plans. Assuming that measured intelligence was inherited, Terman hoped that widespread testing of adults would bring tens of thousands of "high-grade defectives" to government attention.

The ultimate result would be "curtailing the reproduction of feeble-mindedness," Terman wrote, and the "elimination of an enormous amount of crime, pauperism and industrial inefficiency." A better society would result, he suggested, if it prevented "the propagation of mental degenerates."

If Terman's Stanford-Binet test fell short of its author's hard-hearted utopian hopes, it nevertheless became a yardstick, regularly updated, for using questions about vocabulary and logic to assess the mental capacities of generations of

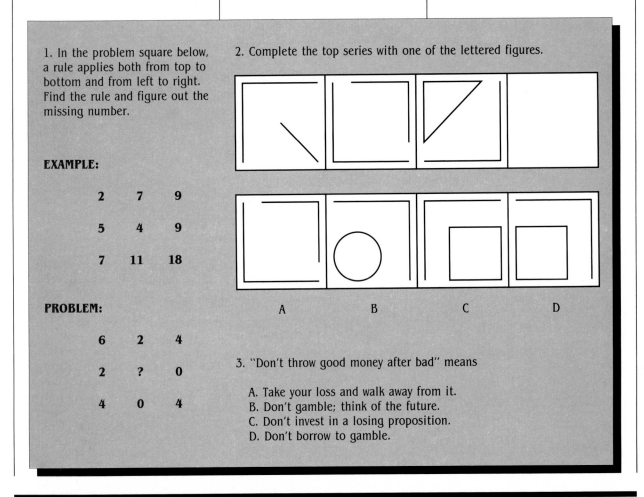

1. In the problem square below, a rule applies both from top to bottom and from left to right. Find the rule and figure out the missing number.

EXAMPLE:

2	7	9
5	4	9
7	11	18

PROBLEM:

6	2	4
2	?	0
4	0	4

2. Complete the top series with one of the lettered figures.

A   B   C   D

3. "Don't throw good money after bad" means

A. Take your loss and walk away from it.
B. Don't gamble; think of the future.
C. Don't invest in a losing proposition.
D. Don't borrow to gamble.

Mensa, an association whose sole criterion for membership is a high IQ test score, regularly collaborates with *Omni* magazine to develop simulated IQ tests. Sample questions from one test appear above. (Answers on page 72.)

Americans. One typical test problem, for example, asks the next number in the series 2, 3, 5, 9, 17 (the answer: 33—each number in the series is arrived at by doubling the preceding number and subtracting 1).

The Stanford-Binet test score is called an intelligence quotient—a quantity derived by dividing mental age, indicated by the score, by the subject's physical age, and multiplying by 100 to eliminate the decimal. Thus, anyone performing at his or her age level would have an intelligence quotient—an IQ, as it came to be called—of 100. A ten-year-old scoring at the level of a thirteen-year-old would have an IQ of 130.

People with IQs below 70 are usually considered mentally disabled—unable to manage their own affairs and incapable of functioning in school or work without special allowances for their condition. Children with IQs above 130 are often identified as academically gifted. For every generalization about IQ and intelligence, however, there are exceptions.

Noting this, many researchers now consider IQ scores misleading indicators of overall intelligence, easily distorted to suggest individual, national, or racial inequality. Standard IQ tests, these scholars argue, fail to take into account other facets of intelligence—creative ability, for example, or social skills, or the special knowledge of the athlete. At best, critics maintain, the tests say something about potential performance in school and in some jobs. But no IQ score, no matter how high, guarantees academic excellence, a brilliant career, or successful adaptation to one's world. □

Meetings of the Minds

One of the burdens of a brilliant mind, according to some extra-bright people, is having to hide it from a jealous world that calls the supersmart eggheads and weirdos. The search for companionable peers seems to explain the popularity of Mensa, an international organization whose only criterion for membership is a high IQ.

Mensa was founded by two British attorneys, Roland Berrill and L. L. Ware, in 1946. Open to anyone who scores in the top two percent on a standardized IQ test, Mensa takes its name from the Latin word for "table," echoing the principle that members are equals. Its original aim was to promote world peace by a fusion of international intellect, and its annual meetings still have large issues on the agenda. Although peace remains remote, Mensa has grown: It has more than 150 chapters worldwide and 80,000 members, 55,000 of them in the United States.

But its appeal has become as social as intellectual. One Mensan, for example, points to "the feeling that, aha, I'm among friends." While most members are white males, membership in Mensa has proved very attractive to women, who describe the society as a place to escape the intellectual shadows of fathers and husbands. According to attorney Joyce Glucksman, one of 900 Atlanta Mensans, the organization also provides a chance to meet brainy males. "It's hard to find men who are not threatened by very intelligent women," she said in 1989. The results of these matches are mixed. The divorce rate among Mensans is high—but so is the number of marriages between people who met at Mensa. □

Debbie Critchley, in what she refers to as her Jewish American Princess costume, and husband Mike, dressed as a farmer, attend a 1990 Halloween party given by Mensa, the organization that brought them together.

His and Hers

Results of intelligence tests show subtle, unexplained differences in the mental performance of males and females. For example, girls usually learn to talk earlier than boys, and women appear to use language more fluently and make fewer errors in grammar and pronunciation than men. But men generally do better at solving such spatial problems as drawing a map of a place they have been or imagining the rotation of geometric shapes. Such disparities have led some researchers to ask whether there are two minds, one male, one female, or a single human mind made different by upbringing and cultural environment.

Recent research has revealed small anatomical differences that, some believe, suggest the existence of two minds. Since men are generally larger than women, their brains tend to be bigger. But in the corpus callosum, which links the brain's two hemispheres, one element—the isthmus—appears to be proportionately larger in women and may strengthen the connection between speech centers.

In men, this view goes, a smaller isthmus would tend to confine the speech function to the brain's left hemisphere. This might explain why, for example, men are slower to recover from speech-destroying brain damage than women and why more boys than girls have dyslexia, a reading disorder in which symbols are mentally transposed.

But many scientists believe that gender-related differences are probably irrelevant. They note that the brains of women and men are far more similar than not and vary within each sex more than they do between sexes. Besides, they say, the mental effects of minor anatomical differences would be undetectable amid the vaster variances caused by cultural influences. □

Lightheaded

"Is Your Brain Really Necessary?" The title of British neurologist John Lorber's 1980 paper got his colleagues' attention. So did his conclusion: a qualified no.

Lorber's main evidence was the case of a student at Sheffield University in England. The young man had a demonstrably good mind: an IQ of 126, a first-class honors degree in mathematics, an ordinary social life. But his brain, the presumed physical residence of his mind, was less than one-tenth normal size—barely five ounces of nerve tissue.

The student's physician, noticing his patient's larger than normal head, had sent him to Lorber, who specializes in brain anatomy. Brain scans showed that the student was hydrocephalic: His cranium was filled mainly with cerebrospinal fluid, leaving a layer of brain tissue near the skull only about $\frac{4}{100}$ inch thick. Lorber had already performed more than 600 brain scans on hydrocephalic patients and had obtained similar results. Many seemed to have unimpaired mental performance; among those whose craniums were 95 percent filled with fluid, half had IQs greater than 100.

This evidence jibed with earlier reports of head wounds that had caused massive loss of brain tissue with no apparent degradation of the mind's abilities. In the early twentieth century, for example, a French boy sliding down a banister fractured his skull on a gas lamp and lost what one witness called "a bowl of brains." After ten days in a coma, he regained consciousness and showed no sign of reduced faculties. One contemporary researcher, citing this and other cases, opined that the brain must serve only to fill the skull.

Lorber draws no such conclusions regarding the brain as the clear locus of mental abilities. What his work shows, he believes, is that the brain, like other organs such as the kidneys or the liver, has a great deal of spare capacity; for the determined mind, a little brain goes a long way. □

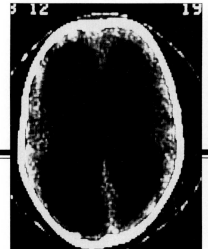 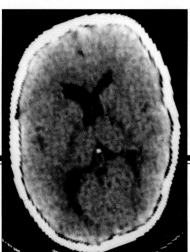

Brain scans of a normal brain *(far right)* and that of a hydrocephalic university student reveal that the young man did well with very little: The only brain cells in his fluid-filled cranium were in a thin layer around his cortex.

Differential Treatment

Roaming the classroom, a spare, middle-aged, middle-sized man hammers away at his audience, taunting them, waving dolls and toy gorillas at them, absorbing their verbal abuse, while pop music booms from loudspeakers. It has the look and sound of improvisational theater, and, in a way, that is what it is. But the performer, Bolivian-born Jaime Escalante, is not interested in entertainment. He is trying, with remarkable success, to deflect a tough Los Angeles neighborhood's young minds toward the difficult mental game of differential calculus.

Escalante uses everything at hand to compel the street-smart adolescents he teaches. The arms of a doll demonstrate the shape of a geometric curve; a rubber gorilla held upside down evokes the idea of a negative coefficient. He forces his students to shout back their answers as he stalks the room with a red pillow used to buffet dullards, then makes deliberate mistakes to allow them to taunt him in return. When enthusiasm dips, he has the students drum on their desks or he switches on the music. For all its turmoil, however, his classroom is the eye of a social storm; outside is the reality of an urban high school plagued by drugs and youth gangs.

From his early days as a teacher in Bolivia, Escalante had been convinced that any youngster with normal mental abilities can learn calculus. After taking some years to earn his California teaching certificate, he became a math teacher at Garfield High School, in a His-

Jaime Escalante teaches differential calculus using such props as fictional alien ET to challenge the underrated abilities of inner-city students at a Los Angeles high school.

panic section of Los Angeles. In 1979, he began an advanced mathematics program there. That year, four of his five students passed a grueling three-hour test to earn college credit for their work.

In 1982, all eighteen students in Escalante's class passed the advanced placement test with such good scores that the testing service suspected cheating. All passed the test again, some with perfect scores, six months later—this time under armed guard.

The success of Escalante's students broke through an entrenched belief in the community that its children's minds simply could not handle something as complex as college-level calculus. As more and more students enrolled in such courses, Garfield's academic standing rose: By 1988, the school ranked in the top one percent of schools nationwide in the number of advanced placement tests taken.

Escalante's unique teaching method depends on his being close to his students. He learns about their personal lives, hobbies, and sports to establish rapport, then cajoles, bullies, and amuses to motivate them to new levels of achievement. The first day of each

class he introduces no math at all, talking instead about the huge posters of basketball stars on the classroom walls. *Ganas*—a Spanish word for "guts"—recurs frequently; he reminds students that they must bring *ganas* to their work in class and at home, to their lives.

The math teacher relies heavily on his sense of the culture of his teenage charges. For example, to spare one gang member from harassment by his fellows, he gave the boy three copies of the textbook: one for class, one for home, and one for his locker, so he need never be seen carrying a book.

Escalante gained national attention in 1988 with the release of a feature film, *Stand and Deliver*, based on his story. But a truer measure of his success was closer to home. That same year, his program enrolled 200 students in seven classes; a second teacher had joined him, and two more, both former students, were being trained to spread his methods. □

Smartski

On the wooded shore of a reservoir serving the Soviet city of Novosibirsk stands a town devoted entirely to improving exceptional minds. Akademgorodok (Academic City) was founded in the 1950s to house the Siberian headquarters of the Soviet Academy of Sciences and to establish a center of excellence in the forbidding wilderness of western Siberia. In later years, a concentration of schools and research institutions grew up, bringing thousands of academics and scientists to the town on the river Ob.

One of the most unusual features of the Siberian suburb is a special scientific boarding school for gifted children. Here several hundred youths study a curriculum that includes Russian literature, history, geography, biology, and English, as well as twenty hours a week in mathematics, physics, and chemistry. Optional courses are taught by outstanding scientists, and students are also encouraged to join research teams at institutes in the town. They work at their own pace: Some of the most brilliant complete the two-year course in one year, while students from less-demanding rural schools sometimes take three years.

The youthful scholars are selected through the National Olympiads, a series of tests designed to elicit evidence of mathematical aptitude. Each October, hundreds of thousands of students submit their answers to problems publicized in schools, newspapers, and youth magazines. About 10 percent, who show originality and creativity in their responses, undergo a round of examinations and interviews during their spring vacations.

Fewer than a thousand youths are invited to Akademgorodok. For three weeks in August, they visit schools and research facilities, attend seminars, and enjoy boating and swimming in the reservoir. At the end of their stay, about 250 are selected to study at the boarding school; the rest are enrolled in a special correspondence program.

The idea of such an exclusive school initially met great resistance from leaders and citizens who feared the creation of an intellectual elite. A stubborn minority within the Academy of Sciences persisted, however, pointing out that children with gifts for science or mathematics should be given the same opportunities as children selected for special schools in ballet, music, art, and sports.

Proponents of the idea won the debate, and the school opened in 1963. It was an immediate success, stimulating students and teachers alike, and generating curriculum materials that were adopted nationwide. A new official attitude emerged that labeled gifted students a national resource. Within a decade, the Academy of Sciences had opened 4 more of the special boarding schools, called *akademgorodoki,* throughout the Soviet Union, and nearly 500 others were started by local education authorities—a commitment to scientific education unmatched in the rest of the world. □

Exceptional Soviet students use the microfilm library in Akademgorodok, established near the Siberian city of Novosibirsk in 1957 exclusively to promote academic excellence in the sciences.

Tuneful Tots

The lively Vivaldi melody coming from the practice room carries no trace of its unlikely source—a tiny violin, scaled down for the diminutive hands of a four-year-old girl. Her face set with determination, she plays the piece from memory with a style that would please a much older player. She seems a prodigy, but, in fact, the girl is just one of thousands of Japanese youngsters trained under a system that assumes any child can learn to play an instrument well if started early enough.

The technique was devised in the 1930s by Shinichi Suzuki, a Japanese violinist and teacher at the Imperial Conservatory. Searching for a way to tutor a friend's four-year-old son, Suzuki theorized that children might learn music just as they do the complexities of speech—by imitating what they hear around them. The system of instruction he developed encour-aged the young mind's inborn linguistic ability, then just assimilating spoken language, to absorb the language of music as well. Because of the way the musical skill is learned, Suzuki called his technique the Mother Tongue Method.

For violin students—who are encouraged to begin before the age of three—the first steps are learning to hold the instrument under their chins and to move the bow. Five simple variations on the familiar tune "Twinkle, Twinkle, Little Star" introduce the first musical principles; only after mastering each phase do students go on to more complex music. Parents attend lessons, monitor practice sessions, and repeatedly play recorded versions of the pieces their children are learning. At about the time they learn to read words, the children begin to read music.

Most students become adept with their instruments (besides violin, Suzuki instructors teach piano, cello, and flute), although

Shinichi Suzuki listens to his Mother Tongue teaching method come to life as he leads 3,000 Japanese violin students in "Twinkle, Twinkle, Little Star" at Matsumoto City Hall in the summer of 1980.

many stop playing in adolescence and few pursue musical careers. Even though there may be no great harvest of professional musicians, cultures that value artistic sensitivity find the time and effort spent in training competent amateurs to be worthwhile. In Japan, some 30,000 Suzuki children are enrolled in a system of 115 schools operated by the Talent Education Institute, headquartered in Matsumoto. And in other schools around the world, 300,000 more are learning music as a mother tongue.

Suzuki believes that his method can work in fields other than music. Every child, he maintains, has enormous potential talents that can be realized only with a proper education—one that begins in infancy. □

Clones Make the Mind

Doron Blake is an attractive blond boy, a bright child with a winning smile and a devoted mother. The only really unusual thing about Doron is how he came to be. His mother, intent on having a baby with a good mind, conceived after selecting his father's sperm from the catalog of the Repository for Germinal Choice.

The repository is a California sperm bank dedicated to improving human intelligence. It was founded in 1980 by Robert Graham, an optometrist who had made millions from the invention of plastic eyeglass lenses. The non-profit organization hoped to collect and freeze sperm donated by Nobel Prize-winning scientists, which would be offered to healthy, mature women who were determined to have smart children and whose husbands were infertile.

The idea that genes conveyed intelligence, and that brighter genes meant brighter kids, was—and is—controversial. Only a few laureates volunteered, most of them over sixty. Within a decade, no Nobel seed remained: The

sperm of older donors is the least able to survive freezing and thawing. The repository's catalog now lists "well-rounded" scientists, smart men with athletic and musical ability, as well as one Olympic medalist. All are anonymous, described by such general attributes as ancestry, height and weight, personality, IQ, and general health. Candidate sperm samples are stored in cryogenically chilled trays and identified with a colored tab and tray number—for example, Red 39 or Burgundy 24.

Among hundreds of sperm banks in the United States, the repository is the only one to screen donors for intelligence. The results are hard to assess, mainly for reasons of privacy. But of the 125 children born by 1990, those in school were reportedly doing well. □

Sperm-bank founder Robert Graham displays one of the cryogenically chilled trays in which color-coded sperm samples donated by intelligent males are stored.

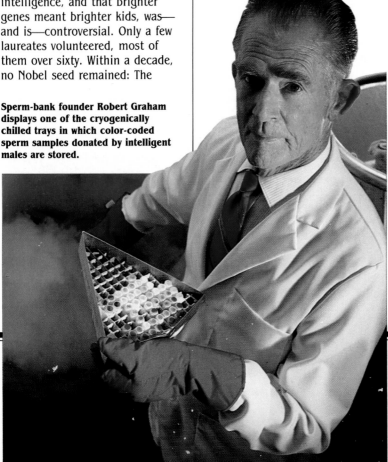

Primeval Patois

Almost from the time that the mind first developed language, scholars have searched for the "natural" tongue from which all others must have risen. Legend has it that an Egyptian pharaoh of the seventh century BC placed two infants in the care of a reclusive deaf-mute to see what language the babies would speak if left to themselves. When they uttered what sounded like the Phrygian word for "bread," the pharaoh decided the original language must have been Phrygian. His conclusion missed the mark, but his experiment did confirm a basic truth: The mind's imperative toward language is so strong that it will create language where none exists.

Compelling new evidence of this has now come from research into languages invented by another group of dispossessed children—languages that linguists call creoles, after the sixteenth-century term for the people imported to

work the plantations of the New World. In fact, according to University of Hawaii linguist Derek Bickerton, creole languages appear to be a kind of modern fossil of that first human tongue.

Creoles arose with the spread of colonialism from 1500 to 1900, as slaves and laborers from diverse cultures were uprooted and sent to such places as the Caribbean and Hawaii. Thrown together with no common language, these workers communicated with invented languages called pidgins—hodgepodges of words drawn from many languages, with no coherent grammar and very little vocabulary. Children raised in such a linguistic melting pot did not adopt their parents' rudimentary patois, however. Instead, they added grammatical structure to the pidgin, creating their own creole language.

Arising in isolation from one another, the world's 350-odd creoles nevertheless exhibit nearly identical grammatical structures, as though they had some kind of common guide. In Professor Bickerton's view, their similarities sug-gest what he calls a "bioprogram" in the mind that shapes the development of language. Theoretically, this inborn set of grammatical rules irresistibly expands crude pidgins into the far more complex and expressive creoles.

But, Bickerton argues, creoles are not merely the created language of displaced slaves: The same syntax appears in the mistakes that all children make as they learn a language. Double and triple negatives, for example, abound not only in creoles, but in the talk of toddlers: "Nobody don't like me." And children, like creole speakers, do not move words around to form questions, relying instead on intonation alone: "You can fix this?" instead of "Can you fix this?" Conversely, children make few errors when dealing with features of their language that resemble creoles.

The first human language, Bickerton believes, evolved from gibberish to pidgin to creole, albeit far more slowly than creole tongues developed among plantation children. As speech emerged in early humans, so did the neural pathways that governed it. Today, these circuits remain as mental vestiges of the earliest ancestral tongue, the built-in apparatus of the mind's powerful impulse to make itself understood. □

Fleeting Fluency

A former United Nations employee named Georges Henri Schmidt *(right)* may have been one of the world's best examples of the mind's linguistic potential. Born in Strasbourg, France, in 1914, Schmidt won French national prizes for translating Latin and classical Greek at seventeen, then went on to study most of the world's important living languages. In 1975, as chief of the United Nations Language Service, he claimed fluency in nineteen: Arabic, Chinese, English, French, German, Japanese, Russian, Spanish, Dutch, Greek, Hungarian, Italian, Persian, Polish, Portuguese, Rumanian, Swedish, Thai, and Turkish. Lack of time, Schmidt noted with regret, had caused him to lose his fluency in twelve other tongues. Like everyone else, the gifted linguist had to use his languages or lose them. □

Too Much, Too Soon

Perfect fluency in a language has always seemed to be the private province of the young, for the mind becomes less able to acquire new tongues as it grows older. During childhood, the business of learning and using language appears to be conducted primarily by the left temporal lobe of the brain, and childhood is the time when learning a language is easiest. Such youthful facility with language may be attributable to the special attention language receives from one section of the brain. By puberty, however, the right side of the brain has begun to take over some of the linguistic work load. This spreading of cerebral labor appears to blur the young mind's sharp recognition of phonemes, the elementary phonetic particles of spoken languages.

But recent work by Canadian researchers indicates that this decline actually takes place long before the onset of puberty. Testing children of diminishing ages for their ability to recognize certain phonemes in the Hindi language, these scientists discovered that linguistic sensitivity was already low in eight-, four-, and even two-year-olds. In fact, it appears that the mind's natural knack for new language begins deteriorating very early in an individual's life: by the age of one.

A decline in sensitivity to foreign phonemes does not necessarily doom the aspiring linguist, however. According to Harvard researchers, adults still learn a second language—vocabulary, grammar, and pronunciation—more rapidly than children do. Adults bring a mature discipline to the task, and they are able to extrapolate words and linguistic rules from the language that they already know. □

Lingua Franca

As the French have always suspected, full fluency in their language exceeds the abilities of most English speakers. The reason is not a matter of national superiority, however, but a basic difference in the way words are listened to on either side of the English Channel.

According to a 1989 study by British psycholinguist Anne Cutler, each language requires a particular kind of handling by the mind to divide the continuous stream of spoken sounds into meaningful chunks. The English mind is tuned to detect uneven stresses on words and sentences and to draw meaning from the way the emphases change. In contrast, French words are evenly stressed, so that the Gallic mind must listen closely not for shifts in emphasis, but to individual syllables.

Apparently, Cutler has noted, the mind's apparatus for developing such listening techniques is quite flexible to begin with but becomes permanently fixed in one mode or the other at an early age. Thus, even comfortably bilingual English speakers are fated to miss many of the subtle cues of native French. □

Tongue Tied

As the mind's instrument of description, language does much to shape one's view of the world. So powerful is the effect of language that linguists once believed it actually altered the way the mind works. As evidence of this, they pointed to the enormous variations among languages used to describe different surroundings.

Languages tend to focus on what is immediate and important—elements that vary drastically from one setting to another. Most European languages, for example, have only a few labels for different kinds of snow. In the Far North, however, the Eskimo have nearly a hundred words for snow, such as *apikak* (first snow falling), *aniu* (snow spread out), *pukak* (snow for drinking water). Similarly, Arabic has many specialized words for camels. American English has more than a dozen words for an automobile (such as sedan, roadster, jalopy), many not even appearing in British English, which is itself filled with terms that mystify American English speakers.

In each of these cases, the language is particularly rich in areas that are especially important to the speakers. There may also be specialization around cultural character: Italian and French, for example, have abundant resources for examining interpersonal relations, while German is well suited for metaphysics.

But however powerful the link between language and the functions of the mind, recent studies suggest that the effect of linguistic differences on mental mechanics is mainly superficial. Even in a language as different from European ones as Chinese, linguistic activity is still strongly centered in the left side of the brain—the same side that processes Western languages.

Another case in point is the

Although it lacks a term for time, the language of the Arizona Hopi is rich with passing days and seasons, as in this naming ceremony wherein a mother and grandmother introduce twenty-day-old Bringing Home An Eagle (one of four names) to the rising sun.

Hopi language of northern Arizona, which, unlike most other tongues, has no word for time; but the Hopi are attentive to days, lunar cycles, and seasons. Even without seconds, minutes, and hours, the passage of time pervades their lives, as it does human existence everywhere.

Thus, while disparities among languages suggest underlying differences in the minds of the people who speak them, these differences do not seem to be fundamental ones. Instead, different languages may be only variations on an innate human grammar, differences that reflect a variety of experience. Language, most scholars now believe, is the voice, not the master, of the mind. □

A Human Chorus

Equipped with an inborn grammar, the mind might be expected to create a single global tongue. But, responding to the shaping pressures of experience and setting, it has gone just the other direction: It has created not one but thousands of languages.

Humans today speak in more than 5,000 distinct tongues and 20,000 dialects. The language with the most speakers is Mandarin Chinese, spoken by more than 700 million people, most of them in China. English is the most globally pervasive: Its 400 million speakers make up at least 10 percent of the population in forty-five different countries. Other languages may be spoken by only a few thousand people, isolated on islands or in remote wilderness areas. In Papua New Guinea, for example, a tenth of one percent of the world's population speaks 15 percent of its languages—more than 700 in all.

Many of these ways of speaking are mainly variations on a theme—the track from English and German to earlier European tongues, for instance, is clearly visible. But many others employ totally different structures. A case in point: Chinese adds to combinations of vowels and consonants a third ingredient, the tone with which the word is spoken, producing an almost musical speech.

The world's most unusual language may be !XU, a clicking tongue spoken in southern Africa. !XU, pronounced as a glottal clicking noise followed by the syllable "zoo," consists of up to eight vowels and ninety-five consonants, half of them rendered as sharp clicks of the lips, tongue, and teeth.

Despite the world's many-tongued cacophony, all speech has certain common threads. In almost every language, for example, the word for mother begins with an *M* sound—the first consonant a human infant can pronounce. □

Flemish artist Pieter Breughel the Elder based his 1563 painting *The Tower of Babel (below)* on the biblical account of God creating languages.

Visible Voices

So strong is the mind's impulse to frame knowledge in some sort of language that, in the absence of one, it will invent its own. Isolated from the sound of spoken words, the hearing-impaired have created literally thousands of alternative languages based not on sounds, but on signs.

Sign languages were probably the earliest forms of human communication and have always been used by the deaf to communicate with their fellows. But the first standardized system of signs for teaching the deaf did not emerge until the mid-eighteenth century in France. The Abbé Charles Michel de l'Épée, a priest who worked with poor deaf children, learned the signs they had improvised to converse among themselves. To these he added new ones that he called methodical signs, intended to enable the silent language to represent French grammatical structure to help the children learn to read and write in French.

L'Épée's method spread throughout Europe and, mainly through the efforts of Thomas Hopkins Gallaudet, to the United States. However, by linking his standardized sign language to spoken grammar, l'Épée had doomed it; the deaf preferred their own individualistic signs. What l'Épée could not have known was that sign languages, by their nature, have little in common with their spoken counterparts. Instead, they are languages designed to be "spoken" with the hands, using eloquent and subtle variations of hand formation and position in space to communicate.

Still, his system had a beneficial effect. At every school for the

hearing-impaired there arose a signing community where different signs that prevailed in different parts of the country were melded into a standardized language. These new systems had their own grammatical forms; the cumbersome methodical signs that forced signing into the shape of spoken language fell by the wayside. American Sign Language, or ASL, which became the standard form in the United States, bears little resemblance to spoken English. Instead of relying on word order for its grammar, for example, ASL indicates sentence structure by facial expression and body movement. It is one of fourteen standardized sign languages in the world, all of them distinct from one another—a deaf Englishman finds ASL as difficult to comprehend as signed Norwegian.

Despite their differences from spoken tongues, modern sign systems are not merely stopgaps, but real languages. Governed by their own peculiar grammar of motion and space, they are as capable as their audible counterparts of conveying highly abstract concepts. Perhaps the clearest measure of their sophistication is the capacity for linguistic wit, including their equivalents of puns and double

Gallaudet University's Gilbert C. Eastman demonstrates that signs (he uses American Sign Language), like spoken tongues, convey rich and often subtle shades of meaning—in this case, three different signs for *open:* open book *(left)*, open window *(center)*, and open mind *(right)*.

entendres. There are plays on signs that look similar but have different meanings. There are also unusual combinations of signs that create new or multiple meanings. Nor is signing without nuance, intellectual subtlety, and emotional resonance. For a deaf person, signs compose the visible voice of memory, reflection, and even dreams. □

Bright Islands

For more than a century, *idiot savant*—from the French *savoir*, "to know"—has described a condition in which the mind is severely handicapped in all but one area, where it performs spectacularly well. The term aptly evokes the bizarre polarity of the rare phenomenon, which one psychiatrist has described as "spectacular islands of intelligence, even genius, in a sea of mental disability." Because almost all known cases are people with IQs above 25, the ceiling for the archaic "idiot" classification, researchers prefer the more modern term: *savant syndrome.*

The effects of savant syndrome are well documented, and doctors know something about whom it most affects. About half of all savants suffer from autism, a mental disorder marked by profound withdrawal and obsessive, antisocial behavior. While some autistics are also mentally retarded, the two conditions are thought to be separate. Savant syndrome is far more common among autistics (about 10 percent) than in the much larger ranks of the retarded (about .06 percent), and more than 80 percent of all savants are male. The areas of remarkable performance are usually quite narrow—mechanical ability, lightning calculation, art, music (usually piano), calendar counting. Occasionally, savants exhibit enhanced senses, such as hearing or scent, or the ability to keep perfect time unaided.

Although theories about the causes of savant syndrome abound, some researchers are looking for a physical manifestation of the disorder in the brain itself. Because a savant's talents are usually those associated with the right cerebral hemisphere, where visualization, spatial perception, and mechanical ability are centered, this search has focused on the brain's left hemisphere, where speech and manual dexterity are dominant.

The left hemisphere develops more slowly than the right one and is thus more exposed to the hazards of pregnancy. It may also be stunted by male hormones circulating in the blood, possibly explaining why most savants are male. Many savants show signs of prenatal damage to the left hemisphere and corresponding enlargement of the right hemisphere. Perhaps, scientists theorize, left-brain deficits force the right brain to overcompensate, switching on flashes of brilliance in the darkness of a mind impaired. □

Model Inmate

James Henry Pullen spent the last sixty-six years of his life in England's Royal Earlswood Institution for the Feeble-minded, near Redhill, Surrey. His custodians had no doubt that he belonged there, but it was they, nonetheless, who dubbed him the Genius of Earlswood Asylum. For Pullen was an artist and master craftsman whose work included ship models so intricate and accurate that they won acclaim wherever they were shown.

Pullen was born deaf in 1835 and never learned much spoken language; until the age of seven, his only word was "muvver," taken to mean mother. His parents, who were first cousins, had one other deaf child among seven who survived childhood (six others died in infancy). The impaired brother also entered Earlswood, where he was a highly regarded artist until his death from cancer at thirty-five. While some doctors believed Pullen's apparent retardation was caused by a brain abnormality, others attributed it to the isolating effect of his deafness.

At five or six, Pullen began carving and drawing his own versions of the toy boats that other boys sailed in the puddles of rutted roads. With obsessive practice, his skill developed rapidly. School, which he attended on and off until he was fourteen, was another story; Pullen picked up a smattering of numbers and words, but he was never really able to read or write.

Admitted to Earlswood in 1850, Pullen went to work in the carpentry shop but proved so superior to the other inmates that he was given his own shop. There he began to produce a stream of meticulously built model ships and houses, as well as furniture, workbenches, and picture frames. He used his limited writing skills to keep a summary of the work in a journal, including the number of pieces of wood used and the amount of money he thought each model might fetch; when he got the chance, he sold some on the sly.

A typical production was a fully rigged wooden man-of-war more than six feet long. Pullen crafted every piece that went into the ship,

Dressed in a splendid, but bogus, admiral's uniform, James Henry Pullen poses with his copper-riveted model man-of-war.

from tiny copper rivets to forty-two brass cannon and a fully operative rigging with 200 miniature pulleys.

Pullen was thirty-five when he began work on his masterpiece, a huge model of the *Great Eastern,* a famous steamship of his day. Ten feet long, it took more than three years to finish, with Pullen again making all the parts from his own careful drawings. The *Great Eastern* was complete in every detail, including anchors and chains, engines, furnished staterooms, and thirteen perfectly modeled lifeboats. A special arrangement of pulleys allowed Pullen to raise the entire upper deck to display the interior. It won worldwide acclaim after taking the first prize medal at the Fisheries Exhibition in 1883.

The near-mute artisan of Earlswood took enormous pride in his craftsmanship; when showing visitors around he frequently paused to pat his own head, muttering "very clever." Usually, however, he ferociously guarded his workshop against outsiders. For one particularly despised attendant, he devised a guillotine-style trap that came perilously close to working. In later years, Pullen tried to scare visitors away with a thirteen-foot-high monster he built in the middle of his workshop. Sitting inside the vaguely human form, he could move its arms and legs and make loud noises through a bugle in its mouth.

At least one stranger, however, completely won Pullen's heart—a woman he chanced to meet outside Earlswood, whom he decided he must marry. Nothing less would do; no argument would dissuade him. He took to moping instead of working. Finally, the hospital staff managed to trick him out of his new obsession. He could leave and marry, staff members told him, but his timing was unfortunate: They were about to commission him an admiral in the navy, with the right to a gorgeous, brass-trimmed uniform with golden epaulets. The offer was too much for Pullen, who quickly altered course. In his remaining years at Earlswood, he wore his bogus admiral's uniform proudly on ceremonial occasions— and never returned to the subject of marriage. □

Calculator's Risk

Louis Fleury, born blind in 1893, was abandoned by his French parents when he was a year and a half old. Placed with a farm family, he developed slowly; at ten he could barely walk and could not wash or dress himself. At a school for the blind in Arras, he had particular difficulty with arithmetic and could not understand division at all. At fifteen, he was labeled uneducable and placed in an institution.

He had been there just two months when a man sitting next to him at dinner suffered an epileptic attack. Fleury had never encountered such a thing and was badly frightened by the fit. To blot the terrible memory from his mind, he concentrated on the hardest subject he could think of: arithmetic. To his great surprise, he easily ran off calculations in his head, even the formerly intractable division.

Unable to convince his custodians that his newfound talent should be nurtured with formal training, Fleury devised a desperate gambit. Pretending to be insane, he tricked his keepers into sending him to an asylum at Armentières. There, the fact that he could engineer such a deception led some doctors to conclude that he was not really retarded after all but that his slow early development had emotional roots. Moreover, they discovered at the hospital, his mind was a powerful calculator.

Released when he was twenty-one, Fleury began to give exhibitions, first in France and then in England and the United States. A typical problem was to express 6,137 as the sum of four squares.

In a little more than two minutes, he gave the answer as $74^2 + 20^2 + 15^2 + 6^2$; ten seconds later he had a second: $78^2 + 6^2 + 4^2 + 1^2$. In another minute or so, Fleury ventured a third solution: $76^2 + 15^2 + 10^2 + 6^2$.

One aspect of Fleury's skill was unique. When he calculated, his fingers fluttered rapidly. Where other numerical prodigies mentally saw or heard the numbers, the blind Fleury was a tactile calculator: He envisioned quantities as imaginary Braille numbers read by his moving fingertips. □

Savant Virtuoso

Applause rolls through the concert hall as Leslie Lemke finishes his spirited piano rendition of *Rhapsody in Blue*. But the slender musician remains oblivious to the audience, sitting impassive before his piano until, at a cue, he launches into another virtuoso performance.

Leslie Lemke is an unlikely entertainer. Blind and palsied, with an IQ of 58, he is severely impaired—except where music is concerned. There, he is little short of a genius. A typical concert ends with Lemke listening to an audience member singing or playing a piece; then Lemke plays it, note for note, mistakes and all, before launching into his own improvised variations on the new theme.

An improbable chain of events revealed Lemke's musical flair. Born in Milwaukee with cerebral palsy and a rare disease that forced the surgical removal of his eyes, he was taken in by foster parents Joe and May Lemke when he was six months old. By age five, his retardation was obvious.

Leslie's speech was limited to repeating the words of others, a condition called echolalia. But he was an inspired mimic, not only playing back every word he heard

during the day, but re-creating the voices of radio announcers, passing strangers, and family members.

May Lemke, a deeply religious woman utterly devoted to her difficult foster child, felt he had an innate sense of rhythm. She bought a piano and was pleased when the boy toyed with the keys. But one night during Leslie's adolescence, May was awakened by the sound of loud piano music. She went into the living room to turn off the television, only to find Leslie flawlessly playing Tchaikovsky's Piano Concerto no. 1—the theme of a movie the family had watched hours earlier. May fell to her knees in awe and gratitude.

With his foster mother's help, Leslie developed a varied repertoire of music from records and radio. Some he could sing, as well as play, in English, German, and other languages; he could also impersonate such distinctive performers as Louis Armstrong. Personal growth accompanied the musical advances, as Leslie learned to dress and eat with little help and to make rudimentary conversation.

In 1974, he began his concert career at a Wisconsin county fair; it would take him to music halls

In their Wisconsin home, May Lemke gives thanks as adopted son Leslie, a savant piano virtuoso and noted concert pianist, plays just for her.

and palaces around the world. May went with him until age forced her to turn her duties over to Mary Parker, her daughter. Despite his social progress, Leslie needs a mediator: When an audience shouts its requests, the titles queue up in his head, and unless someone intervenes, he will play every one, even if it takes all night. □

Prime Movers

Their light blue eyes alert behind thick glasses, George and Charles were identical studies in polite attention as a visitor told them her birthday, March 20, 1938. "That was a Sunday," the twins instantly replied in unison.

For George and Charles, matching days with dates was a simple task. They could do more—naming, for example, the years when April 21 falls on a Sunday or the months of the year 2002 when the first falls on a Friday. But asked to multiply six times three, they might easily decide the answer was eight, or zero, because they are profoundly retarded, each with an IQ of about 60.

They were born in 1939, three months premature; a triplet sister died within twelve hours. They were diagnosed as retarded at age three, and they developed such disruptive behavior that by nine their parents placed them in an institution.

It was there that the twins, who had not been close, became inseparable. George had cultivated the calendar-calculating skill three years earlier, poring over the perpetual calendar in an almanac; now Charles got interested too, though his ability never equaled George's. Proud of their prowess and eager to show off, they achieved brief fame in the 1960s through articles in *Life* magazine and the *New York Times* and occasional television appearances.

In later years, neurologist Oliver Sacks learned that the twins had other talents. For example, once, when a box of matches spilled onto the floor, the twins cried "111" simultaneously, then George muttered "37." Charles repeated it,

then George said it again. Sacks counted the matches—there were 111—and then asked what "37" meant. The twins chorused: "37, 37, 37, 111." Despite their inability to do arithmetic, they had somehow broken the number into its prime factors, 3 and 37.

Pressed to explain how they had instantaneously counted the matches and factored the number, the twins seemed puzzled by Sacks's surprise. They could only say that they "saw" the numbers in a flash. The physician speculated that to the twins, 111 was less a quantity than a descriptive quality, like a color. Their peculiar ability seemed to have nothing to do with calculation. Instead, it was as though, Sacks wrote later, they saw "a universe and heaven of numbers." Left to themselves, they would murmur together, delighting in an exchange of six-, eight-, ten-, and twelve-digit numbers that were all primes—numbers divisible only

Celebrated during the 1960s for their calendar-calculating ability, number-conscious twins Charles *(left)* and George solve problems at the New York Psychiatric Institute, frequently answering in unison.

by one and themselves, and not casually derived. Charles and George were, Sacks believed, "contemplators of numbers."

In 1977, the twins were separated and moved into different halfway houses, where they were able to lead relatively independent lives. But increased social acceptance took its toll. Endlessly jostled by the outside world, their odd numerical communion was shattered and their mysterious ability declined. The twin minds gave up their vast landscapes of numbers, the inner universe that had sustained them for so long. □

Clay Feat

Alonzo Clemons smiled as the elephant sculpture emerged from the clay in his hands. Conversation and explanation whirled around him; television cameras wheeled in for closeups of his work. An audience buzzed with astonishment over the precise detail of the lifelike elephant, modeled from memory in just thirty minutes.

Clearly, Clemons is a gifted artist. He is also severely retarded, with poorly developed speech and an IQ of 40. At age twenty-five, he could barely count to ten, and he had a vocabulary of only a few hundred words, which he used to construct telegraphic responses to simple questions. Born in Denver in 1956, Clemons was a normal, even precocious baby, until a fall at age three left him with brain damage that drastically slowed his development. But somehow his mind preserved a keen early interest in sculpting and continued to develop its rare skill independently, without formal instruction.

Most of Clemons's works are animals, produced from memory. Even a fleeting glimpse at a zoo or from a book can be the basis for a completely accurate replica, down to muscles, tendons, and flopping hair. One observer likens him to a copying machine, rendering perfect three-dimensional representations from two-dimensional pictures.

Clemons's sculptures are valued by art collectors, many of whom are astounded to discover their gifted artist's limitations. His works routinely sell for $350 to $3,000, with some going for as much as $45,000. The proceeds have allowed him to leave a job as a stablehand and buy a house in Boulder, Colorado, next to his parents' home, to use as a studio.

But Clemons's drive to sculpt is a matter of mind, not money; he would continue no matter what the result. Proof of that came years before his success. In 1968, when Clemons was twelve, he entered a residential facility. There, his clay was taken away because his sculpting seemed to obstruct "more productive" behavior. Within a few days, streaks of tar appeared on his bedsheets; under the bed was a sticky menagerie of animals crafted from tar that the irrepressible sculptor had scraped from pavements with his fingernails. □

At the Pam Driscol Gallery in Aspen, Colorado, talented savant sculptor Alonzo Clemons examines *Family Frolic,* one of his many bronzes.

Rain Men

Kim uses a calculator in his work as payroll clerk for a company with eighty-four employees, but only for show. The real calculating of salaries, hours, taxes, and deductions goes on in his head; to keep people from worrying about errors, he pretends to use the calculator.

Facility with numbers is only one of Kim's remarkable skills, which contrast strikingly with the fact that the gentle thirty-eight-year-old is mentally retarded. A so-called savant— one who combines mental disabilities with exceptional talent in a special field—Kim also suffers from autism, a disorder that severely impairs the mind's ability to form relationships and adapt to changing situations. But his combination of ability and impairment made him the original model for the world's best-known autistic savant: Raymond Babbitt, protagonist of the 1988 film *Rain Man*.

Kim (his last name is withheld for privacy) made a strong impression on screenwriter Barry Morrow by reciting all the credits of Morrow's previous films at their first meeting. Fascinated by Kim's memory—which extended to such subjects as history, sports, literature, and geography—Morrow developed a script about the relationship between Raymond Babbitt, a retarded savant, and his normal

brother. By the time the film reached theaters, however, the depiction of Raymond had changed: Instead of concentrating on retardation, the script focused on autism, and Raymond became a composite of many autistic savants.

Actor Dustin Hoffman prepared to play Raymond by spending time with two other models. One, who, like Raymond, lived with a normal brother, remained anonymous. But the other, Joseph Sullivan *(below)*,

won a small measure of fame from the publicity around Hoffman's visits to his hometown of Huntington, West Virginia.

Born in 1960, Joe Sullivan was the fifth of seven children in a well-educated family. He seemed normal and bright as a baby, speaking quite a few words and even singing parts of "The Star-Spangled Banner" before he was two. But by that time it had already become clear that Joe's mind was retreating from ordinary

social interplay, and he was soon diagnosed as autistic.

Locked in his own private world, Sullivan showed periodic flashes of brilliance. At four, he could draw accurate maps of the United States from memory. Later he demonstrated talents for solving complex arithmetic problems in his head and for naming the day of the week for any date, past or future.

One expert likened the skills of Sullivan, Kim, and others like them to the working of an electronic calculator. Although they can perform some specific functions with great accuracy and speed, they are not like calculating prodigies: They have no sense of the meaning of the numbers. Nevertheless, dedicated family and teachers helped Sullivan graduate from high school at twenty-one. His special talents helped him survive the science and math courses and served him well in his subsequent job, shelving books at a public library.

Sullivan's moment in the spotlight arrived when Dustin Hoffman traveled to Huntington for the opening there of *Rain Man*. Kim made it to the Hollywood premiere. Driving from Salt Lake City with his father, he charmed the Los Angeles press corps and restaurant patrons from Utah to California with his *Rain Man* jacket and the loud proclamation, "I am the original Rain Man." □

Eddie's Ivories

Nothing about Eddie Bonafe's early years suggested a hopeful future. His mother was exposed to German measles during her pregnancy, and after Eddie was born in Chicago in 1979, doctors predicted severe retardation and autism. Cataracts nearly blinded him, and even after surgery corrected a heart condition, he remained small and fragile.

Eddie was also deaf in one ear, but his mother detected in him an interest in music, which she tried to foster with a toy piano one Christmas. At first it looked like a mistake. Three-year-old Eddie seemed angry as he banged away with clenched fists. His mother hid the piano in a closet.

Two weeks later, the withdrawn boy spoke his first words: "Mommy, piano, piano, piano." When the toy was retrieved, Eddie began to play all the hymns the family had sung in church that morning. Soon he was playing jazz and pop selections and Latin rhythms acquired in his Spanish-speaking North Side neighborhood. He even played along with the melodies of the TV shows his siblings watched.

A teacher's aide in a class for retarded children brought Eddie's musical talent to the attention of University of Illinois psychologist Leon Miller, providing Miller and other researchers with a rare chance to observe the development of savant skills. Testing clearly showed that Eddie did not simply reproduce music he heard; instead, he understood and remembered its structure.

Nancy Newman, a piano teacher who gave Eddie free lessons, was amazed by his ability. "If you sing a melody to him, he will anticipate the predictable pattern of the melody and add four-part harmony," she reported. "On first listening, he picks up the basic structure of a piece and can reproduce it. But he's also musically creative. He improvises in numerous styles; he ranges over the entire keyboard; he modulates into any key." Under her tutelage, Eddie moved from mimicry to Mozart, as well as other complex classical and popular music. With his vision improved by cataract surgery and thick glasses, he even learned to read music.

Eddie's success with the piano triggered other advances. Affectionate and outgoing, he gave up his frequent tantrums, began to speak well in English and Spanish, and even learned to read. With Eddie's life opening up far beyond her expectations, his mother happily exclaimed, "Eddie doesn't have to grow up to become a musician. He *is* a musician." □

Displaying his mystifying musical talent, ten-year-old autistic savant Eddie Bonafe adds a flourish to an elaborate chord.

Switched Off

Dirty and barefoot, the young panhandler looked like anything but a genius as he asked a startled Oregon housewife for a drink of water. She called the police to come for the hobo, twenty-two-year-old William Troy Landreth, a computer wizard with an IQ of 163. The year before, he had switched off his fine mind and relative success to become a homeless drifter.

Only four years earlier, Landreth had been an underground hero to computer hackers. He was famous at age eighteen as "the Cracker" for his skill at breaking into guarded computer networks.

Landreth had begun applying his brilliance to this arcane trade at thirteen, when he bought his first computer with baby-sitting money. The oldest of nine children, he was left largely to his own devices and soon began spending as much as twenty hours at a time in front of his telephone-equipped personal computer. Soon, from his bedroom in San Diego's northern suburb of Poway, he was picking his way through complex electronic mazes to prowl among Defense Department and NASA files. His stealthy patrols through supposedly secure files attracted the attention of the FBI, which regarded his intrusions as a threat to national security.

In 1983, Landreth was arrested, convicted of wire fraud, and sentenced to three years' probation for using someone else's computer time. At first he took advantage of the publicity surrounding the case, writing a book about his exploits that sold nearly 70,000 copies. In it Landreth professed his credo—that he had broken into computers as an explorer, not a spy. Causing damage was "not only clumsy and inelegant, it was wrong."

Landreth spent two years as a consultant to companies eager to learn how to protect themselves against similar intruders. But one day in 1986, he disappeared, leaving a rambling eight-page essay that ranged over subjects including capitalism and communism, human evolution, nuclear war, immortality, suicide—and boredom. "I was bored in school," he wrote, "bored traveling around the country, bored getting raided by the FBI, bored in prison, bored writing books, bored being bored."

A year of drifting ended in 1987 when Landreth was arrested in Oregon for violating probation. Back in California, he tried to settle down, but when a fire gutted his apartment, he moved to the streets. At twenty-four, Landreth was homeless in San Diego, passing sunny days on a park bench, nights in flophouses or doorways.

Landreth's mother attributed his behavior to manic depression, a diagnosis delivered years earlier in a court-ordered psychiatric exam. His father, a science-fiction writer who had taken the fictional surname of Fourmyle, suffered from the same ailment, which produces wild mood swings. Landreth refused to take drugs prescribed for his condition, complaining that they only made it worse.

Although he seemed to abandon the life of the mind, Landreth remained confident that he could still earn thousands of dollars a day, if he would only do it. "The way I see it, I could be retired in five or ten years, if I did things in a constructive way," Landreth said. All he had to do, he added, was turn on his switch. □

THE GIFT OF TIME

Some simple organisms exist without memory, living from moment to moment. Their world has no history; every experience is virtually new, untouched by the lessons of the past. The human mind, however, has somehow created a memory of extraordinary richness, resilience, and depth. Concealed somewhere in the soft machinery of the brain, memory lives in a landscape of time, fashioning the mind's perceptions of itself, its world, its future. Without that temporal dimension, there can be no real existence. Life would flatten about the mind, holding it eternally in the moment or suspended somewhere in the past. In people whose ability to remember has been tragically destroyed, one sees what the mind has achieved in making such a memory. For without it, and with everything else intact, a keen intelligence will flood with sensory impressions that are unilluminated by experience. Lacking memory, the troubled victim is compelled to endure a life that is drained of meaning by the absence of time.

3

Daughters of the Mind

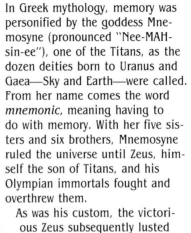

In Greek mythology, memory was personified by the goddess Mnemosyne (pronounced "Nee-MAH-sin-ee"), one of the Titans, as the dozen deities born to Uranus and Gaea—Sky and Earth—were called. From her name comes the word *mnemonic*, meaning having to do with memory. With her five sisters and six brothers, Mnemosyne ruled the universe until Zeus, himself the son of Titans, and his Olympian immortals fought and overthrew them.

As was his custom, the victorious Zeus subsequently lusted after the conquered Mnemosyne and took her as a consort. She bore him nine daughters, the Muses, patron goddesses of the arts. Calliope was the Muse of epic poetry and eloquence, Clio of history, Erato of love poetry, Euterpe of music or lyric poetry, Melpomene of tragedy, Polyhymnia of sacred poetry or oratory, Terpsichore of dance and choral song, Thalia of comedy, and Urania of astronomy. The ancient Greeks understood that behind every creative endeavor lay the mind's ability to remember. □

Personality Quark

Just as physics has its quarks and mesons—basic subatomic particles that nobody has ever seen—so the memory has its engrams. So goes neuroscientific theory, anyway, which posits that memory, however abstract, must make some physical impression on the brain. The hunt for this biological imprint has been long and intense, but few researchers have pursued the elusive engram more persistently than American psychologist Karl Lashley. The researcher at the Yerkes Institute spent years in the 1920s, 1930s, and 1940s teaching rats to find their way through mazes, then incrementally slicing away their brains in an attempt to discover where their memories of the maze were stored.

He found that removing any part of a rat's brain diminished its memory to some extent and impaired its ability to negotiate a maze it had previously learned. But, to Lashley's dismay, he also found that, no matter which part he removed, the rat could still stumble through the labyrinth, some portion of its memory intact. A memory acquired by one of his rats, he concluded, did not dwell in one specific cluster of cells; instead it was somehow distributed throughout the entire brain.

Researchers have since come to believe that Lashley's findings about rat brains apply only in a limited sense to the vastly more complex memory apparatus of humans. Humans' memories seem to be distributed piecemeal among a number of locations in the brain, as rats' memories are.

It is clear, however, that particular parts of the human brain store particular types of memories. This must be so, since the partial destruction of a person's brain eliminates specific memories while leaving others intact. But despite the fact that scientists know where various kinds of memories live in the brain, memory itself still has no fixed address. □

Memory Merchant

In 1902, thirty-one-year-old Marcel Proust's health began to fail, causing the young Parisian writer-about-town to retire to a quieter life—a life that would be spent largely in reverie. Eleven years later, Proust published the first of a fifteen-volume series of novels called *A la Recherche du Temps Perdu*—"in search of lost times," later published in English as *Remembrance of Things Past.* A masterpiece of French fiction, it may be literature's greatest celebration of human memory.

As this tribute to the remembered past begins, the narrator has a sensory experience that transports him mentally back through time, flooding his mind with recollections of childhood. The sensation that triggers this encounter with his past is a simple one, all out of proportion to its dramatic effect. While savoring the combined tastes of a *petite madeleine* (a small, shell-shaped tea cake) and a cup of tea, he discovers that the distinctive

flavor of the hot beverage mixed with cake crumbs recalls a similar taste treat he enjoyed as a boy, when in the village of Combray his great-aunt allowed him to taste a madeleine dunked in her cup of tea. All at once, reported Proust's protagonist, "the whole of Combray and its surroundings, taking shape and solidity, sprang into being, town and gardens alike, from my cup of tea."

Although few can evoke the mind's penchant for memory with Proust's skill, most people have experienced something of the kind, a sensation in the present that unexpectedly conjures up images from the past. The phenomenon is sometimes called a Proustian epiphany. Scientists do not understand precisely how the mind forms such links between past and present or whether the remembered past is the real thing. It is entirely possible, they note, that even Proust's powerful memory searched less for lost times than for times that might have been. □

Neural Electrification

From the 1930s to the 1950s, influential theories about memory arose as a kind of by-product from operations performed at the Montreal Neurological Institute by brain surgeon Wilder Penfield. Looking primarily for the degree of damage caused by epileptic seizures, Penfield used the opportunity to study the mind itself. Once a patient's cortex was exposed, the doctor was able (with the patient's permission) to prowl about the organ, gingerly prospecting for functions. Since the brain itself feels no pain, he could apply electrodes to the exposed neurons and administer small doses of electricity—while the subject remained conscious and able to answer questions.

Penfield's electrical stimulation caused his patients no physical discomfort. It did, however, produce a range of vivid sensory impressions. Stimulating one region of the brain caused patients to hear sounds, stimulating other regions produced involuntary body movements, and so on. Penfield took careful note, mapping the sites of different functions. But then he made a startling discovery: When he applied his electrodes to the temporal lobes, located behind the temples on both sides of the brain, his patients reported sudden memory flashes, often of long-forgotten moments. When he restimulated the same point, the same memory recurred.

A fourteen-year-old patient recalled a bizarre event. As she was walking through a field with her brothers, a strange man came up behind her. "How would you like to get into this bag with the snakes?" he asked. Despite the Freudian overtones of her vision, Penfield was able to confirm that the incident had really happened when the girl was seven. Other stimulated patients heard, or remembered, music, a family moment, a long-past conversation, all wrapped in the emotions of that past moment.

At first, it appeared that Penfield had found the physical apparatus of memory that had eluded his American contemporary, Karl Lashley *(pages 74-75)*. "There is a permanent record of the stream of consciousness within the brain," Penfield wrote in 1959. "It is preserved in amazing detail. No man, by voluntary effort, can call this detail back to memory. But, hidden in the interpretive areas of the temporal lobes there is a key to a mechanism that unlocks the past and seems to scan it for the purpose of automatic interpretation of the present."

There may have been a key, but Penfield never found it. Perhaps, some researchers believe, the engramlike traces animated by his probes were merely part of a vast, redundant inner tapestry of memory—not specific, exclusive sites. In any case, the hidden mechanism he discerned, if it exists at all, still hides somewhere in the mind. □

Montreal neurosurgeon Wilder Penfield mapped the cortex by probing exposed brains electrically, verbally guided over uncharted cerebral terrain by fully conscious patients.

Feelings

Memory has been likened over the centuries to several kinds of recordkeeping, from inscriptions on a wax tablet to patterns of electrons stored on computer chips. But, far from being a purely objective record of experience, memory is intimately entwined with subjective feelings and attitudes. Otherwise, everyone would recall an event in exactly the same way. In fact, each mind retains its own unique recollection. Emotion makes the difference.

Sigmund Freud, the father of psychoanalysis, took early note that emotions have the power to distort, suppress, fragment, and even fabricate memories. For many years, Freud's ideas on this subject were largely disregarded, as scientists who studied memory embraced the notion that memory worked like a camera or a computer, storing information with an almost mechanical objectivity.

Today, however, most theorists maintain that, to be fully operative, the ability to remember must offer the mind not simply a link to the past, but a link to feelings about the past. The mind may remember, but the filter of emotion shapes the memory and, to a large extent, how the memory is used. □

Soft Traces

Remarkable as human memory is, it has its flaws. It is not entirely accurate, for example—and it does not always tell the truth. Studies have shown that recollections are often sketchy approximations of reality rather than fully rendered images. When they are remembered, they are partly recalled and partly imagined. The mind, it appears, brings back a general outline of past experiences but fills in details based on attitudes, assumptions, and beliefs. Memory, according to this view, does not passively repeat the past, but actively reconstructs it.

A leading proponent of this theory was British psychologist Frederic Bartlett, a Cambridge professor who conducted experiments in the 1920s and 1930s to test the reliability of people's recollections. He found that mental images of the past did not compose a solid, consistent record of reality, set down in what researchers then called traces. Instead, they were quite malleable and could be altered and manipulated.

In a 1932 study based on Bartlett's work, Brown University psychologist Leonard Carmichael and two colleagues showed the same simple drawing, a diamond shape inside a square, to two groups of subjects. He told one group that

When two groups were shown the same figure *(above, left)*, the group told that it showed curtains reproduced it as a window *(center)*, while the group told that it was a diamond drew a lozenge *(right)*, suggesting that memory is swayed by preconceptions.

they were seeing a picture of curtains in a window. To the other group he described the drawing as a diamond in a rectangle. A week later, when the two groups were asked to draw what they had seen, people in the first group added curved lines suggesting curtains, while people in the second group drew a small diamond-shaped jewel floating in the rectangular frame.

From this and similar tests, Bartlett concluded that the mind remembers an object or event by making what he called a schema, a kind of composite picture based on the totality of past impressions. In the case of the window-diamond drawing, people did not just store the pattern; they combined it with what he had told them about the picture and linked it to their previous knowledge about windows and diamonds. When asked to recall the drawing, they created a memory based on this schema. "Some widely held views have to be completely discarded," Bartlett wrote, "and none more completely than that which treats recall as the re-excitement in some way of fixed and changeless 'traces.' " □

Moscow Method

The Russian director Konstantin Stanislavsky revolutionized the art of the theater with a form of realistic acting based on "emotion memory" of deeply felt moments from an actor's own life. Before Stanislavsky, performers had relied on mnemonic devices to learn long speeches and remember hours of blocking, or stage movement. But at the Moscow Art Theater, which he cofounded in 1898, Stanislavsky demanded that his actors push beyond such conventions to re-create real, remembered emotions.

Thus, it was not enough for his players to act cold or tired or sick or joyful; he wanted them to reach into their minds, draw forth moments of actually feeling such sensations, then relive the truth of those moments in front of the audience. His actors could not merely wipe their brows to indicate heat, bang their fists to signal rage, or shriek to denote fear—

those were mechanical stage clichés that only gave the audience information about feelings. Stanislavsky wanted the audience to experience the feelings themselves, and he believed his memory-based technique—known as the Stanislavsky Method, or often simply Method—could endow performances with emotional authenticity.

Stanislavsky and the generations of directors and acting teachers influenced by his work devised exercises to help actors recall specific physical sensations and exact moments of peak emotional intensity. Some of these help recapture a physical condition. For example, a woman who has to simulate nausea on stage might use a sense-memory exercise in which she recalls a time when she felt truly sick to her stomach. As she summons up this sensation from her memory, she pays close attention to the ways her body responded at

the time. This gives her a repertoire of physical actions—swallowing hard, puffing the cheeks, and other signs of nausea—that she can use to re-create queasiness in her own body and communicate it convincingly to her audience.

Other exercises help reconstruct a remembered state of mind. An actor who has to weep in a sad scene might use an emotional memory exercise in which he recalls an event that made him cry in real life. He describes the event carefully to a partner, mentioning specific details until he hits upon one that brings tears back to his eyes. It may be something minor— the hairdo on the nurse who brought news of a parent's death, the flowers on a restaurant table where a lover announced the end of an affair—but once the actor has found its emotive power, he can take the memory on stage to conjure up a flow of tears. □

A leading proponent of the acting technique called Method, mentor Lee Strasberg guides students at New York's Lee Strasberg Theatre Institute through an exercise in recalling past sensations.

Telling Tales

In many cultures with strong oral traditions, storytellers have mastered the art of reciting hours of narrative stored in their minds. To dip into their remarkable talent for replay, these traditional tellers of tales—whether Greek poet, European bard, or African griot—use certain mnemonic techniques developed over centuries of decanting remembered songs and stories.

Rhyme, rhythm, and repetition are the three *R*'s for many oral reciters, who use them to create patterns and associations that make narrative material more memorable. Homer's recurring references to "rosy-fingered dawn" in the *Iliad* and the *Odyssey* are a familiar example of a repeated expression that helps to break a narrative into segments for easier memorization and recitation. The same technique is evident in the popular story "The Three Little Pigs" when the wolf delivers word for word the same threat to each pig: "I'll huff and I'll puff and I'll blow your house down." Such refrains and catch phrases divide a story into parallel episodes, thereby easing the task of remembering the story and preserving the narrative flow. The same can be said of the time-honored opening and closing lines of countless fairy tales: "Once upon a time . . ." and " . . . happily ever after."

Alabama-born storyteller Mary Carter Smith, since 1983 the official griot of Baltimore, never tells her stories exactly the same way, but she anchors each tale in her memory by learning the first and last sentences by heart. The rest of the story she remembers in outline form as a list of key points to cover in her recitation. She keeps a file of index cards with notes about each story, but she never refers to a written source when she recites. She listens to new stories repeatedly and reads them over and over to impress them on her memory. She estimates that all the stories stockpiled in her mind would take a good twelve hours to tell.

Bocaccio, a Maryland storyteller who has taken the name of the fourteenth-century Italian writer, commits the events in a story to memory by drawing an imaginary map of the action. As he tells the tale, he moves from one mental landmark to another.

For Washington, D.C., storyteller Jon Spelman, recalling and reciting a story is a visual task. For

Storyteller Mary Carter Smith *(right)* and her husband, Eugene T. Grove, greet her new effigy at the Great Blacks in Wax Museum in Baltimore, Maryland.

example, to remember Lewis Carroll's poem "Jabberwocky," which is full of comical nonsense words, he relies on visual images that go back to his own childhood. The poem deals with hunting a mythical monster in the woods, so Spelman stimulates his memory of the words by using a mental picture of the woods near his boyhood home in Ohio. "Storytelling is a narrative art," he says, "but words aren't really what it's about. It's really about pictures. Words are the medium for translating my pictures into the audience's pictures." □

The Memory Machine

Scientists have never cracked the puzzle of how the mind turns perceptions and experience into memory. Somewhere in the brain's complex electrochemical slurry of neurons, they believe, lies a physical trace of mnemonic activity—something like an engram, the long-sought basic element of memory *(page 74)*. Thus far, that trace has eluded them. However, experiments with humans and animals have begun to reveal what may be memory's faint footprint in the labyrinth of the brain.

Part of this almost imperceptible trail lies in a well-established difference between short-term and long-term memory. Short-term memory is the mind's familiar temporary filing system, lasting long enough, for example, to remember a recently seen phone number for the time it takes to

dial it. This contrasts with long-term memory, which preserves scenes (and even phone numbers) over protracted time—from childhood into adulthood, for instance. Researchers believe that all new information first enters the short-term memory, whereupon some mental mechanism determines whether it should be discarded as transient or stored permanently.

The responsibility for transferring newly acquired knowledge into long-term memory appears to rest with two small curved regions of the brain called the hippocampi (*hippocampus* is Greek for "seahorse"), which lie roughly between the ears toward the base of the skull. The discovery of this came in a 1953 medical incident that has since become famous: the surgical removal of both hippocampi from an epileptic patient identified only

as H.M. *(page 87)*. One result of this operation, which has never been repeated on a human, was the destruction of the man's ability to form new long-term memories. Because he can remember nothing for very long, doctors have concluded that the hippocampi are crucial to acquiring new memories. That conclusion has been supported by other cases involving damage to the hippocampi.

But the actual mechanism of remembrance—whether the memories be brief or lasting—seems somehow tied to the electrochemical communication between individual brain cells, or neurons. It is known that the buildup of electrical charge in a neuron causes the cell to "fire," releasing chemicals that can potentially affect thousands of adjacent neurons. Recent experiments suggest that a sensory jolt produces memory by actually altering the physical structure of the neurons, especially the cells' branching signal receivers, the dendrites. For example, according to University of California neurobiologist Gary Lynch *(left)*, an infusion of calcium causes dendrites to somehow become more sensitive, creating a memory by strengthening the brain's neuronal structure. Other scientists believe that such structural reinforcing is tied to a protein called kinase C, which stimulates the release of many neurotransmitting chemicals, the messengers that pass along information and input from neuron to neuron. Parallel hypotheses abound. As yet, however, no one claims more than an intimation that something biological happens when the mind remembers. □

For many, the shock of seeing the fatal explosion of the space shuttle *Challenger* on January 28, 1986, created an indelible, highly detailed snapshot—what some scientists call flashbulb memory.

Faded Snaps

Many people describe very sharp, detailed memories surrounding events that greatly shocked or saddened them. For example, some claim to remember vivid minutiae from the moment when they first learned of the 1963 assassination of President John F. Kennedy: where they were, what they were doing, who gave them the news, what happened immediately before and after. For many older people, hearing about the bombing of Pearl Harbor in 1941 was such an unforgettable moment. Members of a younger generation have reported the same experience with the 1986 explosion of the space shuttle *Challenger.* Because such recollections are reportedly burned into the mind like photographic images, scientists call them flashbulb memories and propose that they must involve a distinct, sharper type of memory function.

But the phenomenon may be more myth than memory. Psychologist Michael McCloskey and his colleagues at Johns Hopkins University explored just how sharp a picture the mnemonic flashbulb really takes. Querying a group of people about the *Challenger* explosion within a week of the disaster, and repeating the survey nine months later, the researchers found that this kind of memory was neither highly detailed nor permanent. Instead, the seemingly indelible memories etched by shock or grief tended, like ordinary remembrances of things past, to fade and change with time. □

Eyewitness testimony may have led to a historic miscarriage of justice in the 1921 murder-robbery trial of Nicola Sacco and Bartolomeo Vanzetti *(foreground, second and third from left),* who were executed in Massachusetts in 1927.

False Witness

Memory is not well defined, like a mental filing system, but protean—and malleable. It changes and it can be tricked. Numerous studies have shown that people's recollection of witnessed events can be altered and distorted with relative ease to create false memories.

In a 1974 experiment at the University of Washington, for example, psychologist Elizabeth Loftus showed a videotape of an automobile accident, then questioned the viewers about what they had seen. She found that when she asked, "How fast were the cars going when they *smashed* into each other?" people gave significantly higher speed estimates than when she asked, "How fast were the cars going when they *hit* each other?" Their knowledge about the meaning of the word *smash* influenced their thinking about the collision they had seen, leading them to

"remember" a high rate of speed.

Later, when Loftus asked her subjects if they had seen any broken glass scattered on the road at the accident scene, those who had been asked about a smash were far more likely to say yes than those who had heard the milder term, hit. In effect, the mind had imposed a false memory on its perceptions of the event.

Ironically, although the malleability of human memory has been well established, eyewitness testimony continues to carry great weight in the courtroom. Juries tend to trust the memories of witnesses who come across as honest, impartial, and confident of the facts. But memories can be manipulated, accidentally or with intent to deceive, with horrifying results. Innocent people have been imprisoned for years on the basis of mistaken identification by eyewitnesses who thought they were telling the truth. And many believe that

manipulated eyewitness memory has caused at least two wrongful executions, those of Nicola Sacco and Bartolomeo Vanzetti, convicted in 1921 of robbery and murder in Massachusetts, partly on the basis of eyewitness testimony. The two were found guilty and executed, even though other eyewitnesses swore that the accused were elsewhere at the time of the crime. □

Silent Running

In 1969, eight-year-old Eileen Franklin witnessed something so horrifying that her mind effectively forbade her to remember it. Her repression was not in itself unusual; the mind often locks away unendurable memories. Psychologists who have worked with victims of

torture, for example, have found that burying the memory of a cruel ordeal often serves as an emotional survival strategy. But in Franklin's case, the unthinkable thing forced its way back into her consciousness with savage suddenness. One day in 1989, she said later, she gazed into the eyes of her own five-year-old daughter and was swept back twenty years—to the time she had seen her father rape and murder her best friend.

In the hills of suburban San Francisco, the grown Eileen Franklin-Lipsker recalled, she had watched in abject horror as her father, firefighter George Franklin, sexually assaulted eight-year-old Susan Nason, then picked up a large rock and killed the girl with crushing blows to the head. He had warned his daughter that nobody would believe her if she told what she had seen and threatened to murder her as well if she gave him away. Susan Nason's remains were found hidden in a ravine ten weeks after her death, but her murder went unsolved. For the next two decades, the only witness to the crime grew to adulthood, her memory of the killing buried beneath a debilitating mass of fear. When the memory surfaced in 1989, Eileen Franklin-Lipsker took it to the police.

Although her testimony met with initial skepticism from officials, physical evidence supporting her charges gradually coalesced into a case. George Franklin was arrested, tried, and in 1990 convicted of first-degree murder—the only person ever brought to justice in a criminal case on the strength of a childhood memory, long repressed. □

Eternal Youth

Sergei Sergeivich Korsakoff, (below), the great nineteenth-century Russian psychiatrist who pioneered the humane treatment of mental patients, studied a memory disorder that now bears his name: Korsakoff's syndrome. The illness is marked by an inability to form new memories and by a tendency to fill the resulting memory void with confabulation, or fabrication of events. Often, the memory loss is retrograde, erasing not just present memory, but decades of past memory as well.

Caused by failure of the liver, which eliminates toxins in the blood, the disorder is often brought on by alcohol abuse. Alcohol destroys the so-called mammillary bodies of the brain's limbic system. Chronic consumption of the toxin can also cause malnutrition, in particular a deficiency of vitamin B_1. Korsakoff's syndrome may also be associated with meningitis, lead poisoning, or reduced oxygen supply to the brain.

Some patients with the affliction forget most of their lives; others lose a few years and become permanently stuck at some point in the past. One middle-aged victim could remember nothing after 1945, although he had not developed his amnesia until about 1970. Well into the 1980s, he believed he was a nineteen-year-old veteran of World War II. He could occasionally produce a stray recollection from the decades after the war, and he showed some ability to retain a faint memory of new experiences. But for the most part, he was trapped in the past, full of plans for his postwar life. Shown his own image in a mirror, he became confused and agitated: The middle-aged man gazing back at him was not the sanguine youngster he expected to see. □

Memory Masquerade

In 1892, when Helen Keller was just twelve years old, she wrote a story called "The Frost King" for the director of her school on his birthday. Noting how remarkable it was for a child who was both deaf and blind to compose such a visually vivid tale, he had it published in the school's alumni magazine. Soon after it appeared, however, someone pointed out to him that the work was simply a retelling of "The Frost Fairies," published some thirty years earlier by Margaret Canby. The discovery brought a storm of criticism and accusations of deliberate plagiarism.

Upset and baffled by the tempest, Keller tried in vain to recall some contact with "The Frost Fairies." She had no memory of ever having been exposed to the story, yet it was clear that her own tale was a copy and not the original work she had imagined it to be. But Keller *had* "heard" the Canby story several years earlier: A friend had spelled it out to her in sign language against the palm of her hand. Keller's extraordinary mind had retained the story but had forgotten that it was a memory.

Known as cryptomnesia, the innocent masquerade of remembered work as original creation has figured in a number of cases in which scholars, writers, and composers have unwittingly filched ideas from each other. Oddly, cryptomnesia also cuts the other way: Some forget that an insightful flash is actually a memory of earlier work—their own. □

Blind and deaf, young Helen Keller unwittingly published another author's story—one read to her and seemingly forgotten—as her own.

Bourne Again

In the middle of January 1887, a preacher named Ansel Bourne withdrew several hundred dollars from his bank in Providence, Rhode Island. Then he climbed aboard a horsecar bound for nearby Pawtucket—and vanished. Newspapers published notices of his disappearance. Providence police, suspecting foul play, sought unsuccessfully for clues to his whereabouts.

But two weeks after Bourne's sudden departure from public view, a man using the name A. J. Brown arrived in Norristown, Pennsylvania, some 300 miles to the southwest, where he opened a shop and made a living selling fruit, candy, stationery, and other small items. Brown attended worship services, made a number of business trips to Philadelphia, and lived for about six weeks as an unremarkable but well-received newcomer in the community.

One morning he woke up and demanded to know where he was and how he had got there. He had never heard of A. J. Brown, he insisted when his new friends and neighbors tried to talk with him. He had never been a shopkeeper. He was Ansel Bourne of Rhode Island, and the last thing he remembered was visiting his Providence bank to make a withdrawal. His life in Pennsylvania as A. J. Brown had vanished from his conscious mind without a trace.

A fugue, as an amnesia episode such as Bourne's is called, is a rare phenomenon; amnesia is almost never a factor in missing-persons cases. Probably brought on by an overwhelming desire to flee from some kind of stress, a fugue is a type of "hysterical dissociation" characterized by the shedding of ordinary identity and, sometimes, the adoption of a new persona. Most fugues last for only a few hours.

In his more protracted fugue state, Bourne escaped from his life by the drastic expedient of forgetting who he was. He constructed a new identity for himself and hid out inside this alternate self until he was ready to reemerge. No doctors ever pinpointed what happened to trigger Bourne's fugue in the first place or to snap him back to reality eight weeks later. It is known, however, that this was not the first curious incident in Bourne's life. An atheist in his youth, he had converted to Christianity at twenty-nine after a mysterious episode in which he went temporarily deaf and blind, then regained his hearing and sight as if by a miracle. He was also subject to frequent headaches and depression and occasional spells of unconsciousness.

After emerging from the fugue state, Bourne reported retaining no memory of the other life he had created for himself. But he was able to recall the Brown persona while in a hypnotic trance, which suggests that his mind was recording memories during the fugue even though those memories were not available to Bourne's conscious mind. It appears also that Brown had some access to Bourne's memories: Addressing the congregation of his church, he had referred to incidents from Bourne's life. □

Man of the Moment

Because memory of the past is, for almost everyone, an integral part of life in the present, it is hard to imagine what life would be like without this particular faculty of the mind. To live forever in today, utterly without links to yesterday—such a condition is all but incomprehensible. Yet a few people are condemned to just such a life, exiled from the stream of time.

Clive Wearing, a distinguished British musician and scholar specializing in medieval and Renaissance music, suffered a bout of viral encephalitis in 1985 that destroyed his hippocampi—the two seahorse-shaped organs in the cerebral cortex where long-term memory is processed. The illness left him superficially unchanged. His emotions are intact and he greets his wife, Deborah, with every expression of happiness and affection each time he sees her. He retains his full intellectual vigor and still commands all the knowledge and abilities acquired before the inflammation killed part of his brain. But the loss of his hippocampi robbed him of the ability to form new long-term memories.

Now, when his wife leaves the room, he forgets that they have just been together. If she comes back even a few minutes later, he welcomes her as a long-lost love from whom he has been separated for ages. His world is what he sees; when he looks away, it disappears until he looks at it, and re-creates it, moments later. He fills a journal with endless repetitions of the same entry: "Now I am completely

Unable to remember that he knows how to play the piano, musician Clive Wearing is always surprised that he can play for his wife.

awake, for the first time in years." When he reads one of these entries shortly after writing it, he does not recognize it and denies being the author of the words in front of him. He grows angry if anybody points out the similarities in content and handwriting between a journal entry he is making in the present and one made in the past. He has enough short-term memory to concentrate on a game of solitaire, which he learned to play before his illness, but he would not be able to learn a new game. No matter how many times the rules of a new game are explained to him, they can never take root in his mind because his memory cannot process new information.

"Clive's world now consists of a moment," Deborah Wearing says sadly, "with no past to anchor it and no future to look ahead to." But, with heavy irony, his condition takes one further cruel twist: With neither past nor future, he cannot learn what has happened; even as his loss is explained to him, the explanation is forgotten. Trapped in a world without time, suspended in the moment, he knows only that something is terribly, incomprehensibly wrong. □

De-filed

In the course of speaking or writing, people frequently encounter what psychologists call the tip-of-the-tongue syndrome. They cannot quite come up with the word they want to use next, though they know that the word is in their vocabulary. Often, they can summon up a partial memory or a mental clue about the word; they know its first letter or they can hear a rhythm in the mind that tells them how long the word is or how many syllables it has. Try as they may to grasp it, however, the word they want hovers just out of reach.

In the 1960s, Harvard University psychologists Roger Brown and David McNeill began experiments that used the peculiar mnemonic gap to gain a better understanding of how memory is organized. They were led to their study by experiencing a tip-of-the-tongue episode involving the word *Cornish*, remembered variously by them as *Congress*, *Corinth*, and *Concord*. Trying to remember the address of a relative, they found themselves in the situation described by pioneering psychologist William James. "The state of our consciousness is peculiar," James wrote in 1890. "There is a gap therein; but no mere gap. It is a gap that is intensely active. A sort of wraith of the name is in it, beckoning us in a given direction, making us at moments tingle with the sense of our closeness and then letting us sink back without the longed-for term."

In their exploration of this "intensively active" gap in memory, the two researchers supplied experimental subjects with definitions of uncommon terms and asked them to produce the defined words. Whenever this process threw a subject into a tip-of-the-tongue state, Brown and McNeill wrote, "he would appear to be in a mild torment, something like the brink of a sneeze, and if he found the word his relief was considerable."

About half the time, subjects were able to state correctly the word's first letter and number of syllables. Sometimes they could also identify the final letter, the location of the primary syllabic stress, and other aspects of the word they were groping for. Producing strings of words associated in their minds with the target word, they were able to say in each case whether the word they had come up with was similar in meaning or sound to the one they wanted. In analyzing the results of this study, Brown and McNeill likened the memory to an elaborately cross-referenced filing system in which words are grouped according to a variety of attributes.

The word *despot*, for example, might be grouped in the memory with two-syllable words, words beginning with *d*, words ending in *t*, and words of similar meaning, such as *tyrant* and *dictator*. According to this model, a word on the tip of the tongue has been recalled by the "generic memory," which identifies groups of words, but eludes the "particular memory" that pinpoints individual items in a generic grouping.

According to Brown and McNeill, the tests suggest that the mind stores each word not as one distinct item, but as a set of clues that can be used to recall the word. Because some features of a word, such as its first letter, are more prominent in the memory than others, they serve as handles the memory can grasp to retrieve the entire word. But sometimes they are not enough, and the word they evoke is not fully recalled. Instead, it hangs just out of reach—on the tip of the tongue. □

Selfless

By giving the mind a set of connections between past and present, memory establishes the continuity that is essential to personal identity. Amnesia, the loss of memory, destroys those vital links: When people lose their memories, they are deprived not only of their remembrance of things past, but of their sense of who they are in the here and now.

Amnesia can take many forms. It may be brought on by a variety of causes—a blow to the head, disease, surgery, alcohol abuse, emotional trauma. It may last a few minutes or endure for a lifetime. A person with amnesia can lose contact with memories from the past or can lose the ability to form new memories in the present and store them up for the future.

In a case studied by British researchers in the 1960s, for example, a patient known as K.F. was in a motorcycle accident that damaged part of his brain and destroyed a specialized memory faculty, the prompt recall of sounds. K.F.

does not have total amnesia and can comprehend much of what goes on around him, but he cannot take in new information aurally. If he hears a phone number, he remembers only the last digit.

H.M., an epilepsy patient who lost both hippocampi and other memory-linked brain areas to surgery, lives with even more severely impaired memory function. Where K.F. has lost prompt recall for information he hears, H.M. cannot create new memories out of the data from any of his senses. Everything fades from his consciousness as quickly as it registers. Although he actually scored better on IQ tests after his surgery than before, H.M.'s amnesia left him so perpetually disoriented that he lost the capacity to function normally in daily life. He can learn a new motor skill—moving a stylus through a maze, for example—and "memorize" it with his muscles, but his

mind retains no memory of having learned anything. No matter how many times he sees the maze, he always declares that it is entirely new to him. As he moves the stylus through the correct twists and turns, tracing the route that he has traced many times before, he marvels at his good luck in solving the maze on his first try.

A blow to the head or similar physical trauma can produce amnesia of a limited sort. The trauma victim may suffer either posttraumatic amnesia, the inability to remember events just after the trauma, or retrograde amnesia, a loss of memory about events that preceded the trauma. A severe psychological shock can induce memory loss as effectively as a physical trauma. Researchers have studied a few cases in which people responded to emotional stress by temporarily forgetting who they were, losing all recollection of their past lives, and assuming new identities to replace what lost memory had taken with it. □

Déjà Everything

On a tour of England, the nineteenth-century American author Nathaniel Hawthorne wrote of one unusual sight he visited, "I was haunted and perplexed by an idea that somewhere or other I had seen just this strange spectacle before." Hawthorne could not put his finger on the source of this peculiar mnemonic experience, but he commented on "that odd state of mind wherein we fitfully and teasingly remember some previous scene or incident, of which the one now passing appears to be but the echo and the reduplication." As is often the case, the French had a term for the phenomenon: *la sensation du déjà vu.*

Déjà vu, which means "already seen," is a memory illusion, and a virtual opposite of amnesia. Where an amnesiac forgets things that happened in the past, a person experiencing a flash of déjà vu (the sensation rarely lasts longer than a few seconds) remembers things that seem to have happened but really have not. Researchers have no universally accepted theory to explain what causes déjà vu, but many explanations have been advanced over the years.

Freudian analysts have suggested that the phenomenon may involve actual recall of memories that have been repressed and driven out of the conscious mind. Doctors have implicated various organic conditions in the brain. Some believers in reincarnation have argued that déjà vu experiences are glimpses of past lives. Believers in extrasensory perception have suggested that people experience déjà vu when they have foreseen a given situation in a vision or witnessed it telepathically by tuning in the perceptions of another person.

Psychologists who prefer more mundane explanations ascribe déjà vu to a momentary glitch in coordination between the two hemispheres of the brain, which normally receive information from the senses simultaneously. According to this theory, déjà vu occurs when the hemispheres slip out of sync so that half of the brain processes an experience a split second later than the other half. This blurred perception, psychologists say, produces an echo effect that turns the reality of a first-time experience into the illusion of a memory.

But no explanation yet proposed fully accounts for this universally experienced sense of alreadiness. Nor is it just a visual perception. Researchers have described and analyzed nearly two dozen other members of the déjà vu family, including those shown at left. There is even an opposite state of mind, called *jamais vu* (never seen), in which a person fails to recognize a situation that should be familiar from experience—that *has* been already seen. □

Besides the well-known *déjà vu,* psychologists use an entire family of less-familiar terms to express the sense that something in the present repeats something in the past, as in *déjà* ...

arrivé: already happened
connu: already known (subjectively)
dit: already said
entendu: already heard
éprouvé: already experienced
fait: already done
goûté: already tasted
lu: already read
parlé: already spoken
pensé: already thought
pressenti: already sensed (as in a presentiment)
raconté: already recounted
rencontré: already met
rêvé: already dreamed
senti: already felt or smelled
su: already known (intellectually)
trouvé: already found (or encountered)
vécu: already lived
visité: already visited
voulu: already desired

Foiled

In 1960, a man recorded in medical lore only as N.A. was a young air-force recruit whose roommate liked to work out with a miniature fencing foil. As the swordsman practiced a thrust one day, N.A. unwittingly turned toward the oncoming point of the blade. The foil penetrated his nostril and struck through to the brain.

The damage wrought by this mishap left N.A. with global anterograde amnesia, a condition that effectively strands him in 1960. In his fifties during the early 1990s, N.A. remembers his life before the accident, but he has acquired no new knowledge since then. He peppers his speech with the slang of the period, which for him has never gone out of style. He has difficulty locating his San Diego home of many years, and he forgets the plot of a television show whenever the action breaks for a commercial.

Because nothing is remembered, each moment disappears as soon as it is past. By destroying his mind's ability to accumulate new memories, the sword thrust thirty years ago cut N.A. off forever from the continuity of life. □

Short Circuits

In 1978, New York neurologist Oliver Sacks received a man he calls Dr. P. as a new patient. A noted music teacher, Dr. P. had been referred by an eye doctor after reporting visual hallucinations.

There was nothing wrong with Dr. P.'s eyes, but the visual areas of his brain were malfunctioning, causing him sometimes to see human faces on inanimate objects and sometimes to gaze blankly at friends and associates, unable to recognize them. At one point, he removed his shoe for the doctor, then seemed baffled when asked to put it back on: He had forgotten which object was his shoe and which was his foot. When he was ready to put on his hat and leave, he took hold of his wife's head, as if trying to place it on his own. When Sacks handed him a glove and asked him what it was, he deduced that it was a container of some kind, but could not comprehend the suggestion that it might be a container for some part of his body.

Dr. P., whose case was made famous by Sacks's *The Man Who Mistook His Wife for a Hat,* literally could not identify most of the people and objects in his everyday life. He suffered from visual agnosia, a breakdown in communication between visual perception by the eyes and visual recall by the memory. It is caused by a tumor or by degradation in the visual part of the brain. He could recognize geometric shapes and prominent facial features. But he had lost the ability to assemble details into recognizable patterns: He could remember a large nose, but not a face. His world had become almost entirely an abstraction of fragmented minutiae, seen but not understood. Visually at least, his mind had come to function like a computer: It had lost its ability, wrote Sacks, to judge. □

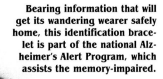

Murdered Memory

Like the brain it lives in, memory may grow ill, weaken, and die, destroyed by one of a legion of diseases that seem cruelly tailored to erase the mnemonic stuff of identity. Despite popular views to the contrary, the enemy of memory is not time. Although the mind's speed may decline with age, most mental tasks can be performed with great efficiency through a normal life span. Thus, some 85 percent of American adults have little or no loss of memory or other mental functions in old age.

The remaining 15 percent, however, suffer some degree of what is called dementia, a loss of memory that makes the aging process particularly heartbreaking. Dementia is seen by the medical profession not as a distinct illness but rather a set of symptoms—primarily the decay of memory, reasoning, and other intellectual abilities—that can be brought on by many maladies and conditions. Creutzfeldt-Jakob disease, Huntington's disease, multiple sclerosis, Pick's disease, multiple strokes—all attack the mind's ability to recall and to think. So may brain tumors, alcoholism, certain infections, thyroid disorders, head injuries, and a host of other afflictions.

But the most pervasive source of dementia is Alzheimer's disease, a form of progressive brain degeneration that affects an estimated 2.5 million of the 4 million Americans suffering from dementia. The disorder usually evolves gradually. At first, the victim becomes forgetful and finds everyday tasks harder to perform. As the disease progresses, the patient often exhibits confusion, behavior change, impaired judgment, and other symptoms of diminished brain function.

Memory, however, is the real target of this plague of the mind. As the disease takes its course, memory disintegrates, and the patient's sense of self begins to unravel, along with the ties of memory that connect individuals to the rest of the world. Dementia erases all the accumulated talent, knowledge, and experience of a lifetime, leaving the individual at the end of life more helpless than he or she was at the beginning. Where an infant's mind eagerly takes in sensory impressions to build its rapidly developing memory, a dementia patient can look neither backward in reverie nor ahead—with the past wiped out, there is little connection with the future. The stricken mind no longer knows itself; the disease isolates it from the flow of human life.

Because so many diseases produce similar dementia symptoms in the old, there is no certain Alzheimer's diagnosis for living patients. It appears that one rare form of the illness is caused by a genetic defect in a single chromosome (number twenty-one of the forty-six human chromosomes). But autopsies of Alzheimer victims have revealed age-damaged tissues and tangles of nerve-cell fibers in areas of the brain known to control memory and intellectual processes. It also appears that Alzheimer's patients are deficient in acetylcholine, a neurotransmitting chemical that is involved in memory. Even with the enemy more or less in view, however, medical science has been unable to discover a way to reverse or heal the brain's deterioration during this cruelest of afflictions. □

Ding!

Medical professionals describe the injury as a mild concussion that produces delayed retrograde amnesia, usually when the head is hit hard enough to produce significant disorientation without knocking the player out. In American football, it is called getting dinged.

The mild concussion, and the transient loss of memory that often accompanies it, is an occupational hazard on the football field, where large bodies in collision create many opportunities for damage. The delayed amnesia takes various forms. In one typical instance, a pass receiver questioned right after he was dinged was able to recall the play his team had just run and could remember the tackle that had knocked him for a loop. A few minutes later, however, he had difficulty remembering any detail of the game, including a hand injury he had suffered on an earlier play. For about half an hour, he could not even remember the padlock combination to open his locker. Two and a half hours after receiving his concussion, he was no longer confused or disoriented and could remember the game events immediately before and after the ding. But he had difficulty recalling the thirty minutes spent on the sidelines being examined and having his memory tested.

In other cases, players examined minutes after being concussed could recall the moment of impact and name the play in which the injury occurred but soon lost that memory permanently. Doctors concluded that a blow to the head may accelerate the fading of newly acquired memories or impede the transition from short-term to long-term memory.

Football is not the only sport where memory-shaking concussion is common, but it is the only one to call it a ding. Boxers, for example, call it "out on the feet." □

Beach Blankness

A healthy man in his late fifties goes to the beach with his family and suddenly, without warning, becomes disoriented and confused. He does not understand where he is or what he is doing. His family rushes him to the hospital, where he has the same lapse of comprehension. He cannot recognize his surroundings and has no idea why he is there. This state, which can last for a few minutes or hours, is sometimes referred to as seashore amnesia because a large number of attacks occur, for some reason, at the beach.

The formal designation is transient global amnesia, and there are a number of circumstances that can trigger an attack. A head injury or migraine headache can bring on an episode, or the memory can blank out if circulation problems interfere with the flow of blood to the brain. Sometimes thought to be a warning sign of an impending stroke, amnesia of this kind does not impair the ability to drive or perform other routine tasks. A person in the throes of an attack remains conscious and can carry on with daily activities in a mechanical fashion, but cannot take in new experiences or form new memories.

After the attack is over, the victim may not remember anything that took place during the period of disorientation. Other memories are unaffected, but the interval of memory failure can leave a permanent hole in the mind. □

Leveled by a hard tackle, San Francisco 49ers quarterback Joe Montana suffers a concussion during a 1986 playoff game against the New York Giants. Such injuries often cause a delayed form of amnesia.

Seeing Things

To recall a scene stored in memory, the mind normally summons up an imaginary reconstruction of the scene originally perceived by the eyes. Some individuals, however, appear to possess the gift of eidetic memory—popularly called photographic memory—in which they seem to actually *see* what they are remembering. According to University of Illinois researcher Ralph Norman Haber, about five percent of American children have this faculty, but hardly any eidetic individuals are found in older groups.

Because many people have strong, well-developed memories, the ability to remember detailed visual descriptions does not by itself prove the existence of true eidetic memory. As a screening device, Haber and other psychologists have devised a number of tests to determine whether memory images are merely detailed or genuinely eidetic.

In one test, subjects are shown a paragraph, then asked to recite portions of the text backward. The task is relatively easy with a photographic memory image in front of the mind's eye, but virtually impossible for someone who has memorized the paragraph in the ordinary, sequential fashion and who lacks eidetic recall.

Another test uses two apparently random patterns, each made up of 10,000 dots, that combine to form a simple picture. Subjects are shown the two dot patterns separately. They are asked to overlay the memory images of the first pattern while looking at the second and describe the resulting picture. Only eidetics can do it. □

To test for photographic memory, a subject studies the top pattern, then visualizes that image while looking at the lower pattern. If remembered eidetically, the two patterns will be mentally superimposed, causing a familiar shape *(right)* to appear.

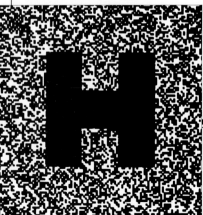

Revered Reverie

The Arab prophet Muhammad, founder of Islam, could neither read nor write. Literacy was not widespread in seventh-century Arabia, and many Arabs prided themselves on carrying long poems and family genealogies in their heads. Accordingly, a tradition of reverence for memorization came to play an important role in the early history of the Koran, the holy book of Islam.

According to Muslim belief, the Koran emerged from a series of divine revelations granted to Muhammad over a period of more than twenty years, beginning in AD 610. As each portion of the unfolding scripture was revealed to him, the Prophet would summon a follower to write down the words of the revelation, while others learned the divine message by heart. Each time, Muhammad gave precise instructions about where the newly revealed verses fitted in the sequence of previous revelations. His followers did not simply memorize the revelations in chronological order, but inserted each batch of new material in the appropriate position among the verses they had already committed to memory.

The written versions of Muhammad's revelations were never assembled in a single volume during the Prophet's lifetime. At the time of his death, the manuscripts were widely scattered, and the Koran existed as a unified whole only in the minds of the many Muslims who knew every word of the scripture by heart. Memorizing the Koran, reciting it, and passing it on to others was an important part of Islamic life. "Reciters" who held the entire text in their memories enjoyed an honored status.

But, during the Prophet's lifetime, seventy reciters were murdered by nonbelievers. A few months after Muhammad's death, seventy more were killed in battle. Such incidents raised the specter of losing the Koran forever. A campaign began to compile an authoritative written version, which was first preserved in manuscript form until it was first published in Istanbul in 1811. Millions of printed copies of the Koran exist today, both in the original Arabic and in translation. But none is more esteemed than the holy book that many devout Muslims still carry in their memories. □

A fifteenth-century French binding holds eighty-six handwritten pages of the Koran set down during the thirteenth and fourteenth centuries. Islamic scripture originally was stored only in the memories of devout Arab "reciters."

Brewmeister

Not everything that memory prodigies store in their mysteriously capacious minds has value. A striking example is Jedediah Buxton, a virtually illiterate eighteenth-century Englishman who could solve complex arithmetic problems and perform impressive—if useless—feats of memory.

Buxton used his calculating abilities to win himself free pints of beer and, as a mnemonic exercise, kept a lifelong mental record of all the free beer he had drunk from the age of twelve onward. For each of the 5,116 pints cataloged in his memory, he could recall where and when he had gulped down the brew, as well as who bought it for him. On one occasion, he received seventy-two pints of beer at a "gathering for his dead cow." Wrote one historian, "I like to imagine Buxton, at whatever ceremony one might have for a dead cow, chug-a-lugging *nine gallons* of beer, while computing such nonsense as the area required for 3,584 broccoli plants."

Lacking the ordinary mental abilities required to lead a normal life, Buxton was never able to harness his remarkable recall to anything more constructive than hustling pints. His memory was much too specialized for general use. For example, taken to see a London production of Shakespeare's *Richard III*, Buxton made no effort to follow the plot of the play. Instead, he counted the entrances and exits of the actors and totaled up the exact number of words spoken by each player. □

Blind Gambits

For centuries, chess masters have displayed an uncanny skill at ''blindfold'' chess, an ability to hold the changing positions of all thirty-two pieces in their minds and play the game without looking at the board. The thirteenth-century Saracen player Buzeccia amazed an audience in Florence, Italy, by conducting two blindfold games simultaneously while playing a third game in the usual manner with the board in front of him.

The annals of chess history and legend abound with stories of players exercising their memories by playing the game in their heads as they eat a meal or enjoy a horseback ride. The eighteenth-century French master François-André Danican Philidor was famous for winning blindfold games even when he granted his opponents an advantage by giving up a knight.

Two nineteenth-century American masters, Louis Paulsen and Paul Morphy, popularized blindfold chess in the United States. In 1857, Paulsen set a record with ten simultaneous blindfold games. By 1900, U.S. champion Harry Nelson Pillsbury had more than doubled Paulsen's record, playing twenty-two opponents at once without looking at any of the boards. Russian-born world champion Alexander Alekhine bettered that record a number of times. His crowning blindfold chess achievement came in 1933 when he played a twelve-and-a-half-hour blindfold exhibition, taking on thirty-two opponents, winning nineteen games, drawing nine, and losing only four.

The current holder of this volatile world record is Belgian master

Blindfold chess wizard George Koltanowski, known as Kolty the Yogi for his powers of concentration, plays an exhibition match at London's Empire Chess Club in 1932.

George Koltanowski, who once achieved fifty wins, six draws, and no losses in nine and three-quarter hours of blindfold play against fifty-six opponents. In his 1955 book, *Adventures of a Chess Master,* Koltanowski described how to do it. Blindfold players, he wrote, use several techniques to hold multiple games in their minds. Some visualize the pieces moving about on imaginary chessboards; others use personal codes and symbols to keep the unseen games clear in their memories. ''The most important thing is to make each game a separate game,'' Koltanowski told a reporter in 1990. ''It's as if there is a light switch in my head so that I know that this is board number seven, that is board number twelve. The most difficult part is to classify each game and know which is which. When I do that, then I can play chess.''

Some memory researchers have theorized that chess masters hold games in their minds by memorizing strategically important groups of pieces rather than storing individual mental images for each separate piece. Because the mind is adept at pattern recognition and retains chunks of related information better than isolated facts, a chess master's insight into the relationships of pieces grouped on the board would help him or her remember the positions of individuals within those groups.

Whatever the mnemonic process, blindfold chess appears to be a long-lived skill. In a 1985 demonstration of memory prowess, Koltanowski invited audience members to call out pieces of information about themselves—phone numbers, birth dates, street addresses, favorite movie stars, and the like. Each fact was inscribed on one square of a giant chessboard until all sixty-four squares were filled. Koltanowski examined the board for a few minutes to memorize the positions of the sixty-four pieces of information, then turned his back and invited a volunteer to pick any square at random. The chess master correctly identified the written contents of that square, then had the volunteer place a knight on the board and move the piece around in its characteristic L-shaped jumps. Guiding the volunteer verbally so the knight touched down on every square of the board, Koltanowski, then eighty-one, reeled off all the names and numbers without a mistake. □

Superconductor

One night as the distinguished Italian conductor Arturo Toscanini was preparing for a concert, second bassoonist Umberto Ventura approached him in great distress. One of the keys on his instrument was malfunctioning, he announced dolefully. He could not play the deep note at the bottom of his register. Toscanini thought for a minute, then reassured the distraught musician. There was no need to worry, said the unruffled maestro, none of the pieces on that night's program contained a bass F sharp for second bassoon.

Toscanini was, as this incident illustrates, not only one of his generation's most gifted musical geniuses, but also a man of prodigious memory. Hampered by poor eyesight, he conducted orchestras without sheet music, relying on his remarkable store of remembered music. He carried in his head every note played by every instrument in 250 symphonic scores, along with the words and music for 100 operas and an extensive selection of shorter compositions. On one occasion, when his orchestra could not locate a copy of an obscure quartet, he wrote out an entire movement of the piece—entirely from memory, although it had probably been decades since he had last laid eyes on the score. But no one is perfect. A later comparison of Toscanini's remembered version with the original revealed that the conductor had made one minor error. □

Poles Apart

The Babylonian Talmud, an ancient collection of writings on Jewish life, law, and belief, was developed from ancient wisdom more than twenty centuries ago in the great academies of Babylon, in what is today Iraq. The 5,894-page text comprises some 2.5 million words.

Originally, tradition forbade writing down the sacred words, so the Talmud's teachings were transmitted orally by scholars who had committed huge quantities of the text to memory. But in about AD 70, as persecution decimated Jewish oral historians, the Babylonian Talmud began to be preserved in written form. With the advent of printing, it began to be reproduced identically, line for line, page for page. Still, the holy text continued to inspire staggering feats of memory—none more amazing than those of a group of nineteenth-century Polish Jews.

The *Shas Polak*, as such a person was called, did more than learn the words of the Talmud by heart. He knew the exact position of every word on every page of the standard printed text. In one popular demonstration of mnemonic ability, someone would open the Talmud and announce a page number, a line number, and the position of a word in the line. After the *Shas Polak* had correctly named the word in that spot, the point of a pin was placed against the word and thrust through several pages of the book. He would then name the word pierced by the pin on any subsequent page. During the entire demonstration, the *Shas Polak* never actually saw the words. Instead, he consulted a mind filled with a kind of photographic record of each page of the Talmud.

But he also showed that remembering and understanding are very different things. These memorizers were not Talmudic scholars and often could not interpret what they recalled. Their ability to commit the Talmud to memory was apparently unrelated to any deep understanding of its meaning. Instead, it appears to have been an intellectual fossil from the days before the Talmud existed in written form—a remarkable ability that survived without the scholarly power that created it. □

Mnemonic whizzes have exercised their talents on the religious texts prized by their cultures. But the record in this field was captured by Burmese prodigy Bhandanta Vicitsara, who in 1974 recited 16,000 pages of Buddhist scripture from memory.

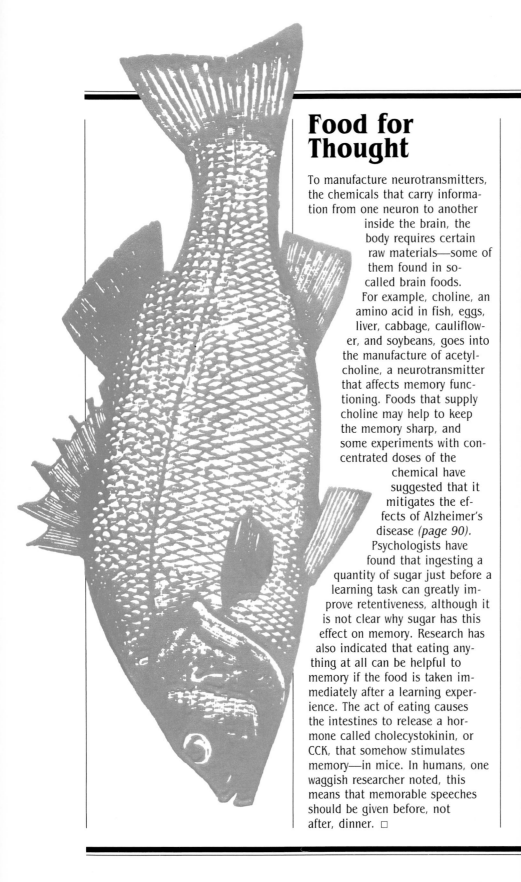

Food for Thought

To manufacture neurotransmitters, the chemicals that carry information from one neuron to another inside the brain, the body requires certain raw materials—some of them found in so-called brain foods.

For example, choline, an amino acid in fish, eggs, liver, cabbage, cauliflower, and soybeans, goes into the manufacture of acetylcholine, a neurotransmitter that affects memory functioning. Foods that supply choline may help to keep the memory sharp, and some experiments with concentrated doses of the chemical have suggested that it mitigates the effects of Alzheimer's disease *(page 90)*.

Psychologists have found that ingesting a quantity of sugar just before a learning task can greatly improve retentiveness, although it is not clear why sugar has this effect on memory. Research has also indicated that eating anything at all can be helpful to memory if the food is taken immediately after a learning experience. The act of eating causes the intestines to release a hormone called cholecystokinin, or CCK, that somehow stimulates memory—in mice. In humans, one waggish researcher noted, this means that memorable speeches should be given before, not after, dinner. □

Junkyard

To have no memory is a terrible affliction, but remembering too much can also be a curse. One spectacular memory prodigy, who was studied for nearly thirty years by the Russian psychologist Aleksandr Luria, displayed virtually total recall of every experience in his life and every piece of information he had ever encountered.

Named simply S in Luria's writings about the case, this master of memory found that his extraordinary retention—a vast web of mental associations tying together disparate bits of information—cluttered his mind and interfered with such intellectual tasks as reading, abstract thinking, and carrying on a normal conversation.

His remarkable memory permitted him, for example, to look at columns of numbers on a blackboard, store a picture of their arrangement in his mind, and later recite them in any order by mentally reading off the numbers in his picture. His recall of information remembered in this fashion was so powerful that it suggested eidetic memory *(page 92)*, but not all of S's recollections derived from what he saw. Because his mind did not recognize strict lines of demarcation separating the different senses, his memory associated the sounds of words with colors, tastes, smells, and textures as well as visual images—a condition known as synesthesia. Every word he heard fit into a complex network of mental patterns and relationships that made it almost impossible for him to lose any item once it had entered his mind. His memory, as an American colleague of Luria's put it, was "a kind of junk heap of impressions."

Because of this inner disarray, S could not generalize from specific experience. When he tried to follow a story being read aloud, he quickly became confused by the multiplicity of images and sensory associations evoked by the stream of words. Thus, while he could rattle off memorized lists of nonsense syllables or foreign words, he could not focus his memory on simple feats of comprehension and recall—hearing and repeating a story, for example—that run-of-the-mill minds take for granted.

As a professional mnemonist, S employed some memory-enhancing tricks of the trade. For example, he sometimes remembered a series of words by using a version of the ancient Greek loci method *(page 104)*. He would convert the words into images and store them along a familiar route; he then recalled the words by mentally strolling along the route and finding the mnemonic images in place.

But his greatest achievement was not in improving his remarkable memory, but in learning to switch it off. Nearly twenty years after beginning to work with Luria, he wrote the psychologist that he had finally made himself forget something. "At that moment," said S, "I felt I was free." □

Using incongruous imaginary objects to mark a mental path for his memory, the Russian mnemonist known as S could recall scenes and events in great detail. But his method was imperfect: Once, when he used an imaginary egg to mark the way, it vanished into a pale wall.

Pi, Pi, Irresistible Pi

In the third century BC, the great Greek mathematician Archimedes became the first person to calculate the value of one of geometry's most fundamental relationships: the ratio between the circumference and the diameter of a circle. The quantity works out to slightly less than three and one-seventh, but never quite settles down—it is what mathematicians call an irrational transcendental number; it can be carried out eternally, in an infinite series of digits that have no repetitive pattern. Archimedes identified the open-ended value with the sixteenth letter of the Greek alphabet: π, or pi.

For most calculations, it is sufficient to use an approximate pi value with just a few digits after the decimal point. Children studying elementary geometry find that 3.14 is good enough for their purposes, while scientists and engineers often employ the more precise 3.14159 for their more sophisticated computations. There is little practical use in calculating pi to any further decimal places—but people do. Besides being important to geometry, pi, it turns out, is an irresistible playpen.

Sir Isaac Newton, the preeminent seventeenth-century English scholar who invented calculus, worked out pi's value to fifteen decimal places and confessed that he was somewhat ashamed of devoting so much time to this diverting but useless exercise. Modern electronic computers have left Newton in the dust, however, calculating pi to hundreds of millions of decimal places. Given the record, it is unlikely that mathe-maticians will quit even if they achieve a billion digits stretching out after pi's decimal point. For one thing, memorizing very long values of pi has become a kind of mnemonic Everest.

A mind to watch in the race to conquer pi is that of Indian memory prodigy Rajan Srinivasen Mahadevan (above), who in 1981 seized the crown by reciting 31,811 digits of pi. Six years later, Japan's Hideaki Tomoyori reeled off 40,000 digits from memory. The deposed pi master enrolled as a graduate student in psychology at Kansas State University, where the National Institutes of Health have funded a study to examine his gargantuan memory. But Mahadevan retains his appetite for pi. Down but not out, he has continued memorizing new digits, hoping to regain his title by reciting pi to 100,000 decimal places. □

Texas Shuffle

It took two hours just to shuffle the cards in preparation for George Uhrin's record-setting memory feat. There were thirty decks in all, a total of 1,560 individual playing cards. After the decks had been mixed, Uhrin (pronounced "wren") spent twenty hours going through the stack card by card, committing each one to memory. He looked at each card only once, then spent nearly three hours reciting what he had memorized. He was able to name all of the cards in order with just two mistakes. This 1989 achievement was enough to win a *Guinness Book of World Records*

citation for Uhrin. The Texas petroleum engineer had failed to set a record a few months earlier when he memorized ten decks of cards with just one error—only to learn that a rival had stolen his thunder by memorizing thirteen decks.

Uhrin first became interested in mnemonic techniques after taking a college course that required extensive memorization. He scoured the library for books on memory improvement and found that visualization was the key to many proven systems. Building on what he read, he created his own memory system, which involves visualizing a series of objects and arranging them in a sequence that he

likens to a movie in his head.

In Uhrin's mind, for example, the four of clubs might be represented as a car with oversize tires, the nine of spades as a mop, and the seven of spades as a person singing into a huge microphone. He deliberately exaggerates some of his visualized objects, such as the tires and the microphone, to make them more unusual and thus more memorable. As he looks at the cards, he concocts a story that links his imagined objects together. To recall the sequence of cards, he replays his mental "movie," which features such combinations as a singer with a big microphone perched on the hood of a car with enormous tires as it drives into a giant mop and gets tangled up in the strands. The deliberately peculiar story serves as an inner map to the order of over a thousand shuffled playing cards. □

George Uhrin, surrounded here by playing cards, memorized the sequence of thirty shuffled decks—1,560 cards in all.

Utter Rote

The modern study of memory began with the nineteenth-century German philosopher Hermann Ebbinghaus, whose 1885 book *On Memory* chronicled years of studies carried out with the author himself as both subject and experimenter. Ebbinghaus wanted to explore what he thought of as memory in its "pure" state, divorced from meaning and comprehension.

He invented hundreds of nonsense syllables—VOD, ZUB, ERK, and the like—and tested his ability to remember lists of these meaningless words. With one reading, he found, he could learn a list of seven nonsense words. To learn a list of twelve, he had to repeat the words to himself fifteen times, and it might take as many as fifty repetitions to learn a list of thirty. While quaint, Ebbinghaus and his experiments have remained influential through more than a century of increasingly sophisticated memory research.

Most modern researchers, however, have little regard for rote learning of the kind that Ebbinghaus practiced to din his strings of meaningless syllables into his memory. Rote memorization, the bane of countless dull and unproductive classroom hours, may be useful for retaining certain pieces of information, they argue, but it is an unnatural mental activity that does not make good use of the mind's higher cognitive abilities.

Still, the mind-numbing techniques of Ebbinghaus and others refuse to go away—and may be crucial to at least one side of human memory. According to University of Pennsylvania researcher Daniel Wagner, studies in the United States and Morocco suggest that rote learning is the best way to acquire reading. "There is growing evidence," Wagner reported in 1981, "that rote learning may be as essential to the learning of the contemporary child as it seemed to our academic forebears of centuries past." □

The Four Major Bodies of Water

PATINA

Pacific Ocean
ATlantic Ocean
INdian Ocean
Arctic Ocean

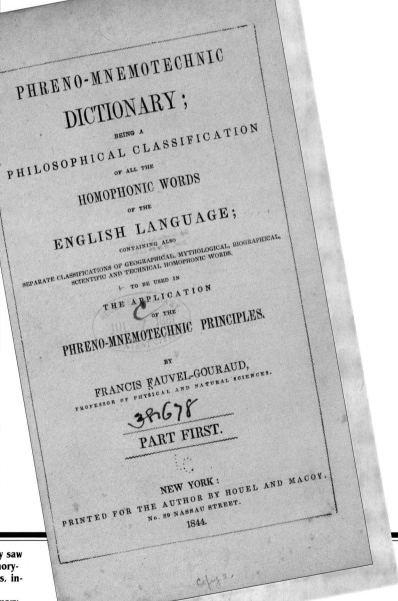

PHRENO-MNEMOTECHNIC DICTIONARY;

BEING A

PHILOSOPHICAL CLASSIFICATION

OF ALL THE

HOMOPHONIC WORDS

OF THE

ENGLISH LANGUAGE;

CONTAINING ALSO

SEPARATE CLASSIFICATIONS OF GEOGRAPHICAL, MYTHOLOGICAL, BIOGRAPHICAL, SCIENTIFIC AND TECHNICAL HOMOPHONIC WORDS,

TO BE USED IN

THE APPLICATION OF THE

PHRENO-MNEMOTECHNIC PRINCIPLES.

BY

FRANCIS FAUVEL-GOURAUD,

PROFESSOR OF PHYSICAL AND NATURAL SCIENCES.

PART FIRST.

NEW YORK:

PRINTED FOR THE AUTHOR BY HOUEL AND MACOY,

No. 89 NASSAU STREET.

1844.

The nineteenth century saw a host of faddish memory-enhancing publications, including this "phreno-mnemotechnic" dictionary published in 1844.

Sweet Memories

The power of smells to evoke memory is not just a literary device or a romantic convention, but an established scientific fact.

In a Yale University experiment, subjects were asked to write out lists of words and were later asked to recall the words they had written. Subjects who had been ex- posed to the smell of chocolate during the initial writing task and again during the recall task re- membered a significantly higher percentage of their words than those who had not received such stimuli. But the aroma of choco- late, pleasant as it may be, does not possess any special mnemonic magic. When it comes to memory stimulation, the Yale experiment found, the smell of mothballs works just as well. □

Placing Faces

The ancient Greeks, who put a high value on the art of public speaking and reciting, considered memory a skill eminently worth cultivating. The first memory-enhancement system, according to legend, was invented by the Greek poet Simonides of Ceos in the fifth century BC, inspired by a fatal accident at a Thessalian nobleman's banquet.

Simonides had sung a lyric poem for the entertainment of the guests when he received a message that called him out of the hall while the revelry was still going on. Moments after he left, the roof of the banquet hall caved in, crushing the diners and drinkers where they sat. Their bodies were battered beyond recognition by the mass of debris on top of them. But Simonides remembered where each guest at the banquet had been seated. By mentally reconstructing their location in the ruined hall, he was able to help the bereaved families identify each body.

It occurred to him that the technique he had used in this case—remembering identities in terms of physical location—could be developed into a formal method for recalling other types of information. He devised a mnemonic system of places and images—*loci* and *imagines*—in which an orator memorized the layout of a familiar house and imagined storing a long oration, section by section, in different rooms. Then, as he gave the speech, the orator mentally walked through the house, finding each part of the speech in its appointed storage place. The technique, called the loci method by modern mnemonists, is still used today. □

ANSWERS TO TONGUE-TIPPERS TEST

1 despot	**9** hemoglobin
2 geode	**10** pterodactyl
3 meridian	**11** geyser
4 venerable	**12** gizzard
5 deciduous	**13** chlorophyll
6 surrogate	**14** yak
7 quintuplets	**15** ventriloquism
8 charisma	

THE CREATIVE REFLEX

The mind is irresistibly an alchemist of ideas. In its recesses, it transforms the ordinary stuff of intellect into treasure: staggering works of art, revolutionary scientific insights, novel sounds, massive feats of engineering. Whole civilizations have risen on the mind's determined impulse to create and collapsed when that uniquely human spark has dimmed. No one knows the real source or limits of creative potential. Even the greatest human talents are bafflingly vague about the wellsprings of their own work. Because tantalizing clues about this godlike faculty have been found in studies of family structure, human development, and even mental illness, many scientists now dream of someday quantifying the creative reflex as they have the modern science of genetics. But so far, the erratic, idiosyncratic code of creativity remains unbroken. The mind does not tell everything, even to itself.

The Gifted

For most of human history, what is thought of today as the creative individual did not exist at all.

The oldest surviving human paintings are cave images at Lascaux, France, and Altamira, Spain. They were painted sometime between 15,000 and 10,000 BC. In all likelihood, however, the artists were considered to be not creative, but inspired. They were shamans, probably helping to guarantee the success of a hunt by the magical device of illustrating it on their cave walls. Even the artists who emerged thousands of years later were not recognized as creators, but were instead anonymous craftspeople who labored on the nameless, routinized religious paintings and funeral art of ancient Egypt.

Only in the era of classical Greece in the fifth and fourth centuries BC was the creative individual set apart—but his (or, more rarely, her) condition was seen as tinged with madness or frenzy, rather than as the product of an innate human impulse to create. Plato even barred poets from his idealized republic because they were not, in his view, responsible people. Still, in the flowering of Greco-Roman civilization, many artists received recognition as gifted individuals—a happy circumstance that soon changed.

In the Middle Ages, the tradition of anonymity once again asserted itself. Although human artistic achievement ranged from dazzling Gothic cathedrals to the splendid ornaments and tapestries of the day, their talented creators were usually known not by their name but by their town, as the master of such and such a place.

Only with the Renaissance did individual creativity become a factor in artistic endeavor. Talent was nurtured in studios and academies. And increasingly, as science uncovered the truths of nature, art became the means of revealing truths about the human spirit. *Genius*, once the name given to the inspirational impulse, was transformed by the eighteenth century to suggest godlike creative powers.

Over the next two centuries, humankind refocused its inquiry into the source of mental originality and became curious about the artists themselves. Genius was localized; it was believed to dwell in a mysterious region first charted by Sigmund Freud: the unconscious mind, the hidden inner studio where artists do so much of their creative work. In the twentieth century, with the spread of universal education and of libraries and museums, the notion grew that creativity was inherent in everyone. Thus in the modern era, *creativity* has become a buzzword and a birthright—not the province of a talented elite, but a democracy of varying abilities. More people lay claim to creativity today than ever before. But the mind's greatest gifts are as rare—and as little understood—as ever. □

Early artists
sketched this bison
on the walls of
the Lascaux Grotto
in France.

Muse of Orléans

By definition, the creative impulse springs from within. But often an external catalyst—a sometimes trivial and out-of-the-way matter—can cause the inspirational juices to flow. The career of Samuel Langhorne Clemens offers a case in point. Long before he, writing as Mark Twain, became one of America's favorite authors, a fourteen-year-old Clemens was inspired by a sheet of paper blowing down the dusty streets of Hannibal, Missouri.

He had quit school two years earlier, after his father's death in 1847, and was apprenticed to a printer. Sandy-haired and fair-skinned, Clemens was a high-spirited and diligent lad who dreamed of travel. Young Sam was known as a good speller, for his printing job demanded it, but he showed little interest in reading and writing and no signs of literary genius. But, one day in 1849, as he was trudging home from work, he saw a page from a book being swept along the street by the wind.

With a printer's curiosity he picked it up and found a leaf from a history of Joan of Arc. The young French heroine was described at age nineteen, imprisoned at the fortress of Rouen, desperately debating her fate with her English foes. Clemens later said that he had felt a deep compassion for the young woman, sharp resentment at her plight, and a sudden interest in history. He became obsessed with Joan and read everything he could about her. His interest expanded to include all of French history, then history in general. Eventually he started to study Ger-

Samuel Clemens at fifteen, a year after he chanced upon a Joan of Arc history that helped shape his later work as Mark Twain.

man and Latin, although he did not go very far with them.

This newly stimulated intellectual interest soon took a literary turn. When his brother Orion founded the *Hannibal Journal,* Samuel contributed to it under the nom de plume of Rambler. He also began writing fiction. When he was seventeen, one of his sketches, "The Dandy Frightening the Squatter," appeared in a Boston weekly. Within a year, he had begun the footloose career that eventually led to an apprenticeship with a Mississippi riverboat pilot, a historic pen name, and the grist for his first major literary work.

But Twain never forgot Joan of Arc, whom he once called "the most innocent, the most lovely, the most adorable child the ages have produced." But his quiet worship of her did not become public for nearly half a century. Then, in 1895, *Harper's Magazine* published as an anonymous serial the work that Twain himself treasured above

all his other creations: *Personal Recollections of Joan of Arc.*

"I like *Joan of Arc* the best of all my books," he wrote, "and it *is* the best," he added, referring to a body of work that includes *Huckleberry Finn. Joan* was also one of the most laborious, taking Twain twelve years to research and two years to write, at times moving him to tears when he recited his heroine's speeches to his family.

Initially, the novel was not well-received. Twain had been afraid of that: The serialization had been published anonymously because he feared hostility to a serious book from readers used to his humor. Slowly, however, acceptance grew, until *Joan* was proclaimed by one of Twain's biographers as "the loftiest, the most delicate, the most luminous example of his work." Twain himself said simply that the book "was written for love"—a chance romance that had begun forty-six years before and kindled his entire career. □

Bachanalia

Occasionally, the creative mind has moments that seem purely miraculous, when new talents or insights seem to manifest themselves suddenly, without warning. Rosalyn Tureck, the world's foremost interpreter of the keyboard music of Johann Sebastian Bach, traces her artistic development to such a moment just before her seventeenth birthday.

Born on December 14, 1914, in Chicago, Tureck was a musically gifted child with promising professional prospects when she went to New York City's Juilliard School in the early 1930s. One day, she recalls, she was learning a Bach prelude and fugue in her practice room, when "I suddenly lost consciousness. I don't even know for how long I was out, but when I came to, I suddenly realized a whole new concept of the structure and meaning of playing Bach."

In simple terms, her musical breakthrough involved discarding the notion of playing Bach's music as if it were separated into right- and left-hand parts and developing a technique based on the independent movement of all ten fingers. "It's as if you have ten hands," she recently explained, "and each must be strong and capable and possess a great deal of control." Her music teacher thought that such playing would require the mind to operate at an impossible level of activity. But Tureck was determined and finally carried the day.

For several years, Tureck taught herself to play the German master's works with the clarity of line, sharply defined rhythms, and intensity of feeling that characterize his music. Then, at twenty-two, she took the music world by storm. Her richly structured, remarkably intense playing sounded, some critics wrote, as if two people were playing two pianos. She subsequently founded the Institute for Bach Studies and the International Bach Society, and wrote a three-volume work on performing the baroque master. She also recorded all of Bach's major keyboard works.

For Tureck, now in her seventies, there has never been the slightest inclination to return to the more conventional techniques of her youth. "I had gone through a small door into an immense, living, green universe," she says. "And the impossibility for me lay in returning through that door to the world I had known." □

Concert pianist Rosalyn Tureck, world-renowned for her inspired renditions of Bach, receives applause from a Barcelona audience at the Palacio de la Música in 1985.

High Art

"It would be vain to try to put into words that immeasurable sense of bliss which comes over me directly a new idea awakens in me and begins to assume a definite form," the Russian composer Pyotr Ilich Tchaikovsky once reported. "I forget everything and behave like a madman. Everything within me starts pulsing and quivering."

Tchaikovsky was not the first creative personality, or the last, to describe a kind of ecstasy in the passion of invention. Political scientist Hannah Arendt called those transports of intellect "thought trains," rushes of simultaneous ideas. Artists have found many ways to describe the sensation, which differs from person to person. "When my brain gets heated with thought," wrote British romantic poet Percy Bysshe Shelley, "it soon boils and throws off images and words faster than I can skim them off."

English Lake District bard William Wordsworth experienced "trance-like states," where the world seemed not quite real, and he suddenly had to steady himself to keep from falling. For Dutch painter Vincent van Gogh, it was a "terrible lucidity when nature is so glorious . . . and the picture comes to me like in a dream." The French composer Claude Debussy, on the other hand, described inspirational moments "when I lose the feelings of things around me," a half-sleeping, half-waking state.

Sometimes the creative high that can transport a genius is visible even to strangers. When the great German composer Ludwig van Beethoven, a short, frail man, was inspired, his whole appearance would change. His eyes would grow wide and roll about, while his physical presence would suddenly seem to expand. "His slight figure, like his soul, would tower before one in gigantic size," as one eyewitness put it. Sometimes the transfiguring inspiration would come to him on the street, startling passersby.

He was not the only composer whose physical presence was altered by the act of creation. Franz Schubert's tone of voice would change when he was inspired. Richard Wagner, interrupted by a friend while composing *Die Meistersinger,* looked "completely changed, almost wild."

But some of the greatest artists have viewed such inspiration with suspicion. French sculptor Auguste Rodin, for example, cautioned against such moments, which "by inducing a condition akin to intoxication" could cause an artist to lose the ability to interpret a subject. And in the view of French novelist Gustave Flaubert, "You should mistrust everything which resembles inspiration." The inspiring moment, such giants argued, was useless without an informed and disciplined mind. □

Impassioned creators Pyotr Ilich Tchaikovsky *(above)* and Ludwig van Beethoven *(right).*

Brain Drain

During the 1950s, American managerial science believed it had an answer for everything—including the mass production of creative thinking. In the cold war theater of ideas, a weapon was needed to outperform Soviet collectivism with corporate creativity. The answer seemed to be: brainstorming.

Brainstorming was the 1950s brainchild of Alex Osborn *(above)*, a New York psychologist and author. He believed that creativity came from the free flow of ideas, a spontaneity that was regulated—or overregulated—by the restraining faculty of judgment. He wanted to systematize the method of Thomas Edison, who often stormed his way toward solutions by trial and error. Edison tried hundreds of substances, for example, before finding the proper filament material for the electric light bulb. To Osborn, the quantity of ideas loosed by Edison looked like a key to group creativity, in which many heads would be that much better than one.

His rules were simple. No criticism was allowed at brainstorming sessions; any idea, no matter how fanciful, was encouraged; and the goal was a large quantity of ideas, from which, presumably, ideas of quality could be culled later.

The technique was widely embraced by corporations such as IBM and bureaucracies such as the army. It produced impressive statistical results: In one case, 89 ideas for reducing absenteeism were generated in thirty minutes; and a group from the Treasury Department brainstormed 103 ideas for increasing savings-bond sales in just one forty-minute meeting. Clearly, brainstorming produced a massive body of ideas.

But further study suggested that the ideas tended not to be very good ones. In fact, brainstorming groups were worse at generating high-quality creative ideas than people working alone. The Organization Man was not necessarily the Creative Man after all. □

Young Louvrers

The most intensely creative period in almost every human's life starts at around age two and has already begun to fade at six. It is the period in which the child's mind absorbs and begins to master the symbols of culture and the elements of true spoken language—a time when it seems that all the possibilities of improvisation come together in fresh and spontaneous ways. The creative distance that children travel in these formative years is huge compared to the distance they will later traverse, unless they are very gifted. As Russian writer Kornei Chukovsky put it: "The young child is the hardest mental toiler on the planet."

He or she may also be the most original, since everything a child does is new. Unforced originality is reflected in the startlingly appropriate figures of speech of very young children—describing a naked body, for example, as "barefoot all over," or reveling in the creation of musical nonsense verse. Children's art has a novelty and unselfconsciousness that many masters struggle to emulate. "I used to draw like Raphael," Pablo Picasso once said, "but it has taken me a whole lifetime to learn to draw like a child."

By the time children are seven or eight, however, they have usually absorbed the main rules of culture, and they consciously begin to observe its constraints. Children become preoccupied with the standards of their peers; spontaneity gives way to conscious conservatism. Paradoxically, just when the natural fountains of

creativity begin to dwindle, a child's conscious appreciation of artistry begins to rise: As they decline as natural artists, children become natural critics.

Increasingly, societies are coming to recognize that there is something rare and magical in childhood creativity that deserves special appreciation. One testament to that recognition is Norway's International Museum of Children's Art, formally established in Oslo in 1986. Containing some 100,000 works originating in 150 countries, the museum aspires to become the Louvre of the very young. □

A colorful self-portrait, *Myself,* by seven-year-old Bilgundi Gurydatta Mallinath of India and a scrap-wire bicycle sculpture made by a ten-year-old boy from Rwanda are part of the growing collection at Norway's International Museum of Children's Art.

Writers' Writuals

Like a baseball pitcher who goes through an elaborate windup before throwing a fastball, the creative mind sometimes demands some highly individual preliminaries before getting down to business. The exact purpose of the rituals is usually obscure, but the rites often seem absolutely necessary to provide the proper blend of tension and security that creative minds appear to need to do their work.

The nineteenth-century French novelist Honoré de Balzac, for example, composed almost entirely at night and put on a dressing gown that looked like a monk's robe before setting to work. When he was embarked on an important project, Irish dramatist Richard Brinsley Sheridan would rise at four a.m. and light large numbers of candles. About 150 years later, Beat Generation writer Jack Kerouac would also light a candle before sitting down to write, then blow it out when he finished.

Chicago Nobel Prize winner Saul Bellow, who says he can only write until one p.m., keeps two old-fashioned Smith-Corona typewriters for his work—one for fiction, one for essays and criticism. They can never be interchanged. He is perhaps unwittingly following the example of the French romantic novelist Alexandre Dumas *père*, who used different colors of paper for different kinds of work: blue for novels, yellow for poetry, pink for journalism. Dumas also used different pens for novels and plays.

For many creative minds, the preliminaries to inspiration involve creating a kind of psychological order. English novelist Charles Dickens *(left)*, whose literary output was huge, could not begin until he had moved the ornaments on his desk into specific patterns. Mark Twain felt comfortable writing in bed. American Nobel laureate John Steinbeck would smoke a pipe, whittle, and engage in the time-honored practice of sharpening pencils before turning to his work. The New England novelist John Cheever, at one low point in his career, would sit naked in a yellow chair in his dining room, smoking cigarettes, drinking whiskey, and meditating on past travels to pry loose his creativity.

Most rituals are aimed to some degree or other at shutting out disturbance. But not all. Storyteller Isaac Bashevis Singer said that he liked best to write sitting in his living room, composing between pauses to answer a constantly ringing telephone. Prolific horror writer Stephen King, who turns out 2,500 words per day, every day, except for Christmas, Thanksgiving, the Fourth of July, and his birthday, says that what sets his creative juices flowing is rock-'n'-roll—fortissimo. □

Master Music

Musical talent tends to appear at an earlier age than any other creative ability, and musical prodigies regularly pop up around the world. None, however, has combined precocity with adult genius in nearly the measure displayed by Wolfgang Amadeus Mozart.

Born in Salzburg, Austria, in 1756, Mozart showed such early promise that his father, a violinist and composer, gave up his own ambitions to further his son's career. Picking out chords on the harpsichord before the age of three, the child memorized and played minuets at four and composed a concerto at six.

By then, young Mozart's powers were already on display before the crowned heads of Europe. On tours that took him to the courts of Austria, France, and England, he played piano, violin, and clavichord while dressed in miniature adult finery that sometimes included a wig and a sword. The Salzburg prodigy charmed his audiences (Austrian Empress Maria Theresa took him onto her lap for a kiss), and he was well-paid. For example, Mozart received 100 guineas, more than $50,000 in present-day currency, for a short public concert in London.

On his return to Austria in 1765, Mozart had already completed ten sonatas and five symphonies, the beginning of a prolific composing career that was cut short by his death at age thirty-five. More than 600 of his works survive, their number and quality nearly defying rational explanation.

Mozart claimed that his musical ideas arose spontaneously as he traveled, walked, or lay awake at

Mozart, shown at the keyboard he had mastered by age seven, toured Europe with his father and sister.

night; he memorized the ones he liked, sometimes humming them to himself. Gradually these tidbits accreted into larger pieces, until a whole work stood "almost complete and finished in my mind." His manuscripts confirm this description: Mozart always penned the primary theme of a piece straight through, often as fast as he could write, then went back and added the subordinate parts.

While most experts agree that Mozart's creativity could only have sprung from an exceptional mind, many now point out that music was, in a sense, simpler then than now: Rigid formulas existed for each type of music. Thus, many important musical decisions were already made, freeing Mozart to concentrate on the brilliant breaks with the accepted that made his music uniquely beautiful. □

Rare Flair

The creative mental faculties that produce graphic art occur only rarely among child prodigies, and those few youthful artists usually have more drawing skill than creative flair. One extraordinary exception is Wang Yani, a Chinese watercolorist whose work at the age of four showed a rare degree of animation and subtlety.

Born in 1975 in a lush, mountainous region of south China, in a house surrounded by tall pines, lotus ponds, and orchards, Yani often accompanied her father, oil painter Wang Shiqiang, on excursions through the countryside and to a nearby zoo. The two amused each other with improvised stories and spent hours spinning fantasies about clouds passing overhead.

Yani's painting began before she was three, when one day she drew with charcoal on a work of her father's, then stepped back to study her own work in a perfect imitation of him. Soon he gave her paper and brush, which she used to paint flowers, trees, animals, and portraits of her father. While he helped Yani discover techniques for moving the brush and handling ◊

paints and washes, Wang Shiqiang was careful to allow her to develop her own style.

By age four, Yani was creating swift, fluid renditions of roosters and her favorite monkeys, which she loved to visit at the zoo. She worked without models, relying instead on her phenomenal visual memory—a memory that permitted her to learn complex Chinese characters by watching her father write them just once with his finger, in the air.

At six, Yani had already produced 4,000 paintings, which were exhibited throughout China; two years later, one was selected for a postage stamp. International acclaim followed, with tours of Japan, Germany, and England by the time Yani was eleven. In 1989, she was the youngest artist to have a one-person show at three of America's most prestigious museums of Oriental art.

Wang Yani's amazing career differs from those of other accomplished artists mainly in one aspect: its incredible speed. Like all artists, she passed through developmental stages such as scribbling and literal rendition. But the talented Yani, in an environment of complete support and enthusiasm, flowered as swiftly as the pumpkin blossoms she paints so well. □

At age four, tiny Wang Yani was painting boldly styled portraits of animals: *Fishing (far right)* was done when she was five, *The Meeting (above)* at nine.

Alexander Calder presents his newly created circus of moving sculptures in New York in 1929.

Perfect Poise

Alexander Calder's carefully balanced, abstract, and often brightly colored works introduced motion as an intrinsic element of sculpture—and, in the process, created a new art form, the mobile. His gradual progression toward sculptures that move is a study in how a creative genius stalks an entirely unprecedented objective, one that nobody has thought of before.

Calder was born in 1898, in Lawnton, Pennsylvania, into a world pervaded by art. His father and grandfather were both sculptors, his mother an accomplished painter. But young Alexander showed little inclination to emulate them. Instead, he enjoyed an ordinary middle-class boyhood, heavily involved with sports and friends. He did exhibit, however, a marked facility for making things with his hands and enjoyed creating jewelry and toys for his younger sister out of wire—precursors of sculpture to come.

Rather than going to art school, he chose to attend the Stevens Institute of Technology in Hoboken, New Jersey, graduating in 1919 as a mechanical engineer. Calder held several engineering jobs before feeling the tug of art in 1922 and taking a night-school drawing course in New York City. A year later, he joined the Art Students' League. In 1924, he began doing illustrations for the *National Police Gazette*, covering prizefights and once, for two weeks, drawing scenes at a circus. In 1926, he moved to Paris, and soon, for his own amusement, he began creating small, movable circus animals and performers out of wood and wire. Now in New York's Whitney Museum of Art, the collection grew into a miniature circus of some fame.

The evolving artist then began to experiment with large-scale wire sculptures, as well as what he called action toys, for exhibition. Among other things, he made an assemblage of wire goldfish bowls that held wire goldfish. When a viewer touched a crank on the mobile, the fish swam in their bowls. It was the first movable sculpture.

In 1930, Calder met the austere modernist Dutch painter Piet Mondrian, whose works, Calder later said, "started" the mobiles. Mondrian inspired Calder to paint. A year later, Calder began creating motor-driven, geometrically shaped sculptures. "The idea of making mobiles came to me little by little," he once said. "I worked with whatever I had at hand." It was the surrealist artist Marcel Duchamp who named them mobiles. By 1932, most of Calder's mobiles were hanging pieces held together by wires and so delicately poised that air currents rather than mechanical devices propelled them.

The first major international show of Calder's work was held at the 1937 Paris World's Fair. His reputation spread rapidly, and he began a procession of success through Europe, culminating across the ocean with a show at New York's Museum of Modern Art in 1943. Calder's works started on a relatively small scale and grew. Finally, they reached monumental size: large, brightly colored, sometimes whalelike shapes hanging in the air or arching up from the ground. By the late 1950s, Calder's reputation as a sculptural giant had been secured. "I make what I see," he said in those days. "It's only the problem of seeing it." He died in New York City in 1976. □

The Road to Guernica

Pablo Picasso was one of the most accomplished painters of all time, and one of the most assured. A child prodigy, he could draw before he could speak. His finished canvases have such virtuosity that they seem to have been spun off with ease, giving little sense of the lengthy thought and creative evolution that went into them. Some of that process is on display, however, in the creation of perhaps his most famous painting: *Guernica (right, below).*

In January 1937, the Spanish Republican government, then beset by the powerful rebel forces of General Francisco Franco, asked Picasso to create a work for the Paris World's Fair. Only a few months later, German bombers gave him an enduring subject. On April 26, a squadron of planes attacked the undefended Basque town of Guernica, leveling it and killing 800 civilians. It was the first massive bombing of civilians in Europe, and Picasso resolved to memorialize the outrage. By May 1, he had completed a number of sketches for the enormous canvas, which measures some eleven by twenty-five feet. A little more than seven weeks later, the work was finished—a virtuoso performance.

But when Picasso died in 1973, he left behind some sixty preliminary drawings, forty-five of which figured heavily in the final painting. The sketches show large changes along the way. A bull that dominates the left side of the final canvas, for example, vanishes and reappears, and its style changes greatly. The position and attitude

of other figures—a horse, a mother and child—also vary. A warrior in one version becomes a broken statue on the finished canvas.

Despite his enormous talent, Picasso had embarked on his masterpiece without knowing exactly where his mind would take him. *Guernica* illustrates more than the horror of total warfare; it shows that even the most gifted practitioner of art must follow an uncertain creative path. □

In the course of designing his chilling masterpiece *Guernica (above),* Pablo Picasso experimented with many powerful images, including the terrified horse in this detail from an early sketch *(top).*

Trivia Pursued

The creative mind, at least in the popular view, is the special apparatus used by writers, painters, musicians, sculptors, dancers, and the like to produce a unique expression of their world. Scientists are generally left out, even though their work is often both creative and unique. As a result, a debate over whether there are two different kinds of creativity—one artistic, one technical—has raged for generations. One school of thought insists that the processes are identical and may even be based on the same kind of judgment. Another, more pragmatic school argues that science deals more in the results of conscious groundwork than inspirational flashes.

No less a scientific original than Albert Einstein testified that the creative impulse in all walks of life is inherently similar. The same view was emphatically invoked before Einstein by the eminent nineteenth-century French mathematician Henri Poincaré, whose assertions derived from his own experience. At one point in his career, the Frenchman was attempting to disprove an elaborate series of equations. He labored daily at the problem for more than two weeks, then set the puzzle aside while he relaxed on a geological excursion to northwestern France. "Having arrived at Coutances," he wrote later, "we entered an omnibus to go some place or other. At the moment when I put my foot on the step, the idea came to me, without any-

thing in my former thoughts seeming to have paved the way for it." The equations in his troublesome series, he realized, were identical to those in an arcane, but known, area of geometry.

Poincaré was so certain of his insight that he verified the results only much later. The solution convinced him that "unconscious work," as he called it, plays the same role in mathematics as it does in the arts. His sense of correctness about the equations, Poincaré felt, was an aesthetic, not a scientific, judgment, based on his own individual "sense of beauty." Other thinkers have compared the judgmental process to rearranging bits of colored glass until a pattern emerges.

Critics point out that Poincaré's "foot on the step" insight underplays the intense intellectual preparation he had undergone for two previous weeks. Rather than an unconscious artistic process, they suggest, the mathematician's inspiration was likely the result of what they call creative worrying, broken only by a change of pace. In other words, his unconscious did not take over; his conscious mind never let go.

Adherents to this view place less stress on inspiration and more on the process of comparing and combining ideas in a kind of ceaseless intellectual friction. Further study seems to bear this out. In one of the most thorough studies of the technical mind ever conducted, Dean Keith Simonton, a psychologist with the University of California at Davis, questioned

2,000 researchers in the late 1980s about their intellectual activities and assembled a number of common characteristics. The study indicated that scientists were generally not the freewheeling innovators artists are. As one researcher put it, scientific work is "tortuous, tentative, enormously complex, and full of unwarranted assumptions."

But the study also shattered a persistent stereotype: the scientist methodically plodding toward the limelight. In fact, Simonton found, the oddest thing about scientists may be their willingness to do huge amounts of work on subjects that seem trivial, often for little gain. Characteristically unafraid of failure, they are daring risk takers—and frequently wrongheaded.

The great sixteenth-century scholar Sir Isaac Newton, for example, reshaped science with his laws of gravity and motion. He also devoted twenty-five years of his life to the futile study of alchemy, publishing thousands of pages on the subject. Alfred Russell Wallace, whose work paralleled that of evolutionist Charles Darwin, used his genius to explore the source of bogus "messages from the dead." And Einstein, who maintained that one creative mind was much like another, gave history an unparalleled example of scientific rigidity. He remained resolutely opposed to one of the most important scientific developments of the twentieth century—statistical quantum mechanics—because it contradicted his deep belief in simple, universal, natural laws. □

Clown Prince

Robin Williams is a unique funny man: a public laboratory of comedic invention. His free-associating improvisations and intuitive leaps into a multiplicity of personalities are legendary for their electrifying pace and hop-skip-and-jump variety. Sometimes they end in comedic pratfalls, but Williams never tarries to examine the results. Admirers compare his improvisational method to jazz. Critics have occasionally compared it to madness.

Williams's humor combines zany personification with playful word associations that lead his characters to say progressively more outrageous things. In rapid-fire order he may spout dialogue as Albert Einstein, a Nazi, an English school headmaster. In the movie *Good Morning, Vietnam,* he played a manic air-force disc jockey who, in a stream-of-consciousness routine, both mocks the irrationality of the war and empathizes with the soldiers who fight it.

He describes his live, stand-up comedy as "a drug"—a form of aggression designed to avoid pain. "You're trying to keep the world out by being aggressively funny, or by mocking it, because somewhere along the line, when you let it in, you hurt," he told an interviewer.

There is little in Williams's own background to suggest the need for such defenses. The only child of an upper-middle-class auto executive's family in Wake Forest, Illinois, he was an excellent student and a highly regarded athlete. His comic inspiration apparently came from his mother, a former actress and model. His father was aloof and something of a disciplinarian. Despite his privileges and attainments, Williams says he was a lonely and vulnerable child who took refuge in a swarm of imaginary characters outside himself.

For all his comedy's apparent edgy effortlessness, Williams says that on-the-spot creativity is also nonstop work. "There'll be moments when you get a spark, a gleam of light, and—boom! You're gone," he has said. "It's like having sex in a wind tunnel." □

Comedian Robin Williams cuts up while preparing to play a neurologist in the 1990 film *Awakenings.*

Only the Only

Psychologists have long sensed that creativity was somehow linked to order of birth in a family and pondered, for example, whether firstborn children are more—or less—original in their thinking than their siblings. In the 1960s, two studies designed to answer such questions pointed in precisely opposite directions. Now, more than two decades later, another research project has turned up a more intriguing wild card: Birth order is less important to creativity than growing up alone.

The new notion about creativity and family position was unveiled in a 1984 University of Hawaii study of fifth-, sixth-, seventh-, and eighth-grade children, many of them gifted, who were tested to analyze their capacity for "divergent" thinking—the kind that enables an individual to break from the pack and search out the new and different. The highest ratings by far went to only children; thereafter scores declined according to whether the child was oldest, second, third, or last in a family.

One explanation for the only child's creative edge focuses on parental attitudes. Firstborn children are welcomed with great joy, much attention—and often, great expectations. When other children arrive, some of that attention is diverted, possibly causing stress for the first child. Elder children are often expected to set a family example in ways that place more emphasis on rules and regulations than on divergence. This may give them a leg up on leadership: As of 1980, 49 percent of U.S. presidents were oldest sons, as were 35 percent of British prime ministers and 38 percent of the world's eminent scientists. But while they have drive and ambition, the eldest children are usually conformists, not apt to be risk takers: Years of setting examples and competing for parental approval take a toll.

Only children, on the other hand, lose none of the parental attention and do not have to be role models. There are evident benefits. In a review of 200 studies, a University of Texas psychologist found that only children tend to be more intelligent, show more autonomy and maturity, and ultimately fare better in life than other children. A higher proportion of noted scientists than politicians proved to be only children or only sons, which some researchers took as a sign of greater abstract creativity in science than in politics.

The study also suggested that middle children do not suffer as much in the family competition as had been thought. Parents are more relaxed with the in-betweens, who are consequently more likely to learn skills of compromise and diplomacy. But middle children tend to choose very different paths from their elder siblings—with middleness comes a strong reluctance to conform. □

Passed On

Most scientists today maintain that there is no such thing as a gene for creativity. They say this despite tantalizing evidence to the contrary: Entire families often exhibit pronounced talent that seems to be inherited.

Such gifted families existed long before there were studies of them. Certainly the greatest musical dynasty in the world was that of the Bachs of Germany. Johann Sebastian Bach was the most distin-guished member of his clan, but no fewer than sixty Bachs wrote at least one musical work, and all twenty of J. S. Bach's children are now considered to have been eminent musicians and composers.

British biologist Charles Darwin's revolutionary work on evolution built to a remarkable degree on theories, attitudes, and interests displayed by his grandfather Erasmus Darwin, a pioneering eighteenth-century intellect. In our own time, the acting Redgrave family of Britain, among others, has displayed notable talent across several generations, as have the painting Wyeths of America.

The first man to attempt to find a systematic connection between genetics and genius was Francis Galton, a British social scientist whose book *Hereditary Genius* was published in 1869. Galton studied 300 families that had produced 1,000 men of eminence. He concluded that the more closely one was related to someone eminent, the more likely one was to be eminent oneself. But in ◊

Galton's day, when breeding created a monopoly of power in a class-dominated society, his study could not be described as scientific in any modern sense.

A survey that began in 1979 at the University of Minnesota approached the task differently. It gave six days' specially designed tests to more than 350 pairs of twins, including sixty-five sets in which one twin had been reared apart from the other. The analysis yielded no sign that a single gene produced creativity but found that up to 50 percent of such qualities as leadership and obedience to authority could be inherited. The need to achieve, including ambition and a taste for hard work toward goals, was also deemed to be genetically influenced.

It may well be that at a minimum, certain physical and neural traits that are indispensable to some kinds of creative talent may be inherited. An unusual sensitivity to nuances of light or sound, for example, would be crucial for a great painter or musician. Certain kinds of mathematical talent, which may be related to the capacities of specific centers in the brain, might also prove to be inherited. Where the creative mind is concerned, however, genes are not everything. Families appear to be just as important as vessels for concentrated influence and the passing on of lore. What most research shows is that exceptional abilities turn up in highly intelligent families where children are involved early in serious communications with adults and their minds are encouraged in early childhood to be creative.

In those circumstances, talent in one generation may well become genius in another. A case in point: In Málaga, Spain, late in the last century, a father named Francisco put down his artist's brushes when his son, Pablo, turned thirteen. There was room for only one genius in the Picasso family. □

Sound and Fury

That the great creative mind works best in solitude is one of the grand clichés of creativity. In fact, the truth of the truism depends on the individual. As myriad examples have shown, many do like it quiet—but some like it loud.

Sir Isaac Newton, for instance, was described as "passionately fond of his quiet," and famed British painter Joseph M. W. Turner felt the same. German philosopher Immanuel Kant could be disturbed by the scratching of a pen, while Arthur Schopenhauer, a German philosopher who came along about a half-century after Kant, compared the cry of an animal to a headsman's ax. Once, when Frédéric Chopin was playing the piano, a servant quietly put a letter on his music desk; witnesses said the composer's hair literally stood on end with annoyance. To avoid interruptions, American inventor Thomas Edison, French novelist Honoré de Balzac, and English poet Robert Browning, among others, simply adjusted their schedules: They worked at night.

But many other great minds have thrived on hubbub. British novelist Jane Austen did her writing in a general sitting room, as did Charles Dickens, who preferred to spin his novels amid the swirling life of a large family. British physicist Lord Kelvin did mathematics aboard railway trains. William Makepeace Thackeray created his Victorian fiction at hotels or in clubs. "There is an excitement in public places," he said, "which sets my brain working." □

Raven Maniac

American author Edgar Allan Poe had one of the most bizarre and striking imaginations of his time. Yet he boasted that fantasy and intuition had nothing to do with his creative methods. His haunting poem "The Raven" proceeded step by step, Poe wrote, "with the precision and rigid consequence of a mathematical problem." He said elsewhere, "The truly imaginative mind is never otherwise than analytic." So eager was Poe to erase any idea of a mysterious creative impulse in his work that he deliberately shaded the truth about how much inspiration was involved in his labors.

He described the composition of "The Raven" in an essay, "Philosophy of Composition," that laid out his notions about planned creativity. The poem's length, 108 lines, he said, grew out of a mathematical notion of the subject's merit. He first considered a parrot as the object of the unhappy meditation but opted for the more impressive black bird. Then, having decided on a mel-ancholy tone for the work, he explained, "it would have been absolutely impossible to overlook the word 'Nevermore' " as a refrain.

Poe also liked to give the impression that "The Raven" was the work of an afternoon. In fact, it gestated for years, with much trial and error along the way. The idea of the raven may have been borrowed from Dickens's contemporary novel *Barnaby Rudge*, in which the protagonist owns a pet raven, rather than from the rigorous analysis claimed by Poe. And he may have lifted the refrain "Nevermore" from another poet, who had used it in a lament for his mother. Moreover, Poe was far from cool and detached while working on the poem. He was often compelled by his insecurity to pester fellow artists for opinions of the work. Why the misleading account? In Poe's day, the poet was a highly romanticized figure, and the hard labors of the creative mind were slighted by a public that chose to believe in pure inspiration. Goaded by the popular belief in instant poetry, Poe—a fine and meticulous craftsman—leaned very far the other way to show that creation means more than art: It is hard work for the mind. □

Piece of Mind

Science has proved that all the instructions needed for biological reproduction and evolution are inscribed in coded messages called genes. Genes are arranged on long strands of DNA, or deoxyribonucleic acid, the building blocks of life. Now, some scientists have begun to wonder if there might not be similar building blocks of thought and creativity. These, they believe, would combine and recombine in an intellectual equivalent of cell division and drive the evolution of human culture. They call such bits of creativity memes.

Derived from the Greek word for imitation, the term was invented in the late 1970s by Oxford University zoologist Richard Dawkins, one of the first to conceive of a mental parallel to genetics. From a biological point of view, evolution is the way that genes propagate themselves over history. Suppose, pondered Dawkins, that human culture proceeds the same way, transmitted aboard infinitesimal structures in the mind. Such fragments of thoughts, persisting for varying lengths of time, would evolve into something else, continually changing to make comprehensible the bewildering chaos of the external world. They would be the building blocks not of life, but of creativity and comprehension.

Dawkins's hypothesis of mental propagation may help to explain the widespread acceptance of tunes, catch phrases, fashions, ideas, even religions and sciences—as well as simultaneous discoveries and golden ages of enlightenment—as the products of meme evolution: Rather than individual products, the earmarks of culture are shared characteristics, based on the hypothetical combination and recombination of memes. Their duration and spread are an index of their evolutionary success. Christianity, for example, might be marked by Dawkins's theory as the cultural sign that a certain set of memes had triumphed.

Sociobiologists Charles J. Lumsden and Edward O. Wilson have taken these ideas even further. If the meme is the equivalent of the gene, there must be something more basic yet, some equivalent of the nucleic acids that are the building blocks of genes. They have called this tiniest piece of mind the culturgen, which forms the basis for broader cultural coding. Rather than preexisting in the mind, argue these researchers, culturgens are created in the process of learning—an idea that might help explain the vagaries of human culture in different societies and the act of creation itself.

A key difference between memes and genes, however, is that the latter can be seen and tampered with, while no one has ever found a meme or a culturgen in nature. No one, in fact, even knows quite where to look. If they are in there, the mind is not telling. □

Khan Do

One of the most famous tales in English literature concerning the magical nature of creativity has to do with Samuel Taylor Coleridge's haunting, unfinished lyric, *Kubla Khan*. In 1816, the author of *The Rime of the Ancient Mariner* published the hypnotic poem as *Kubla Khan: Or, a Vision in a Dream*. Describing its origins, Coleridge told of retiring in 1797 to a lonely farmhouse in Devonshire. As he passed one evening there reading a book called *Purchas, His Pilgrimage*, he felt a little indisposed and took a painkiller. Then he fell asleep, he said, thinking of Samuel Purchas's account of how the Mongol emperor Kublai Khan ordered a great palace and garden to be built, enclosing ten miles of ground. Coleridge slept for three hours, and while dozing, dreamed a poem of 200 to 300 lines. "Images rose up before me as things," he related, "without any sensation or consciousness of effort."

When he awoke, he said, he remembered the entire poem and quickly began to write it down. But just then, in the middle of his efforts, he was interrupted by a businessman from the nearby town of Porlock, who detained him for an hour. Alas, when Coleridge finally returned to his labors, he could recall only a few more scattered lines. The dream had vanished.

For more than a century, Coleridge's story was accepted as an example of a poet's creative unconscious at work. But skepticism slowly grew. For one thing, Coleridge sometimes lied about the amount of time he spent on his creations. He described one 400-line poem, *Religious Musings*, as having been written over a single Christmas Eve; in fact, it had taken two years to complete.

Gradually, it became clear that something similar had happened with *Kubla Khan.* In 1934, a second version of the poem—perhaps an earlier one—turned up, written in Coleridge's hand. It was quite different from the 1816 text. Some of the variations brought the poem closer to the Purchas book that Coleridge claimed to have been reading, and to John Milton's *Paradise Lost.*

The story of how the poem was composed also changed with the earlier version. Instead of being the inspiration of a dream, the poem supposedly owed its origins to "a sort of reverie" brought on by taking a tincture of opium. There was evidence that as early as 1811 Coleridge had talked about a dream palace, although he made no mention at that time of a poem on the theme. Further, although Coleridge kept extensive diaries, there was no word in them of his extraordinary dream. And, addicted to opium, he rarely wrote his best verse under its influence. Most experts now assume that Coleridge labored long and hard over *Kubla Khan*—and that his inspiration dried up before he could finish the poem. It is highly possible that at least some of the images in *Kubla Khan* did come to him in a reverie, lingering until he had time to start crafting them into an elaborate work. But when his imagination failed, he was left with an unsalable fragment—unsalable, that is, unless it could be published as the remnant of a magical dream-revelation, an ultimate epiphany of the poetic mind. □

Rave Reviews

From the time of Aristotle, observers of the artistic scene have sensed a connection between creativity and disorders of the mind. "Those who have been famous for their genius," the ancient Greek declared, "have been inclined to insanity." According to scientific studies in recent decades, the idea is more than just a cliché.

The best-known study is a survey taken by University of Iowa College of Medicine psychiatrist Nancy C. Andreasen during the early 1970s. She studied fifteen top writers at the university's renowned Writer's Workshop and compared them with a control group chosen for similarities to the writers in age, sex, and education. She found that ten of the writers suffered from mood disorders; only two of the control group did. Two of the writers were diagnosed as manic depressive—that is, subject to extreme psychic ups and downs.

Over the next fifteen years, Andreasen continued the study, building the sample to thirty writers. The proportion treated for mood disorders climbed to 80 percent, as against 30 percent for the control sample. More than 40 percent of the artists had been treated for manic depression, versus 10 percent of the others, and two of the thirty committed suicide; there were no suicides in the control group. Thirty percent of the talented sample were alcoholic, against only seven percent of the controls.

Meanwhile, a 1983 investigation by psychologist Kay R. Jamison of the University of California at Los Angeles examined forty-seven important British artists and writers and found that 38 percent of ◊

Almost an archetype of the brooding artist, a haggard Virginia Woolf exudes depression in this portrait made two years before her 1941 suicide.

them had sought treatment for mood disorders—thirty times the rate for the general population. Poets headed the list: Half reported that they had entered psychiatric facilities at one time or another. Two-thirds of the playwrights in her sample had been treated for mood disorders. Visual artists fared considerably better, at 13 percent.

Why do talent and mental illness constitute such a frequent match? Both creative minds and disturbed ones, as Iowa's Andreasen puts it, have "extremely finely tuned nervous systems" that are very sensitive to external stimuli. There is some evidence to show that those who suffer from a depressive disorder use creativity as a means of finding relief from their plight. The manic phase of a manic-depressive cycle, by comparison, often resembles creative activity: Both creation and mania cause a person to exhibit high energy, enthusiasm, intense emotions, alertness, and sleeplessness.

Andreasen has insisted, however, that the resemblance is somewhat misleading. Artists are not their most creative during extreme highs. Even Vincent van Gogh, popularly viewed as reaching the peaks of insanity and artistic creativity at about the same time, did his best painting when well. "Creativity is not linked with *wild* craziness," Andreasen says. Artists brood, but rarely rave. □

Age of Creation

"A person who has not made his great contribution to science before the age of thirty will never do so," declared Albert Einstein, who conceived the theory of relativity at twenty-six. But research indicates he was being too dogmatic. The mind's creative peaks occur at different ages, depending on the challenge. Studies have shown that for chemists and poets, the peak of creativity comes, as Einstein claimed, before age thirty. For mathematicians, symphony composers, physicists, and botanists, the prime years are thirty to thirty-five; for astronomers, philosophers, and opera composers, thirty-five to thirty-nine. Novelists and architects bloom last of all; for them, life *may* begin at forty. □

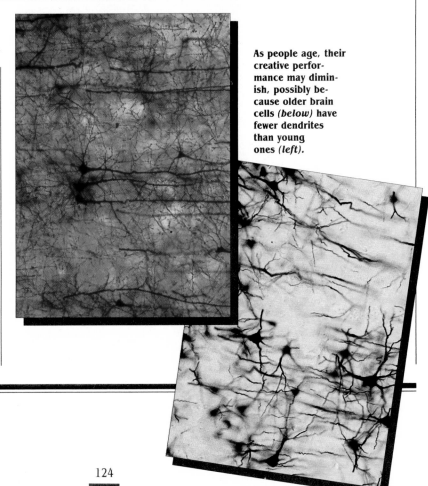

As people age, their creative performance may diminish, possibly because older brain cells (below) have fewer dendrites than young ones (left).

Hatching the Who

Thidwick the Moose. Bartholomew Cubbins. Grinches, Sneetches, Yooks, and Zooks. The seemingly inexhaustible stream of curious characters and rhyming nonsense yarns produced by Theodor Seuss Geisel, known as Dr. Seuss, has made him one of the world's most original and popular children's writers. More than 100 million copies of Seuss's books have been sold. He has won the Pulitzer Prize, along with two Emmy awards for television versions of his work.

Charming and affable, Seuss seems to balk at only one question: Where do his ideas come from? His stock tongue-in-cheek reply: "Once a year, every August, I hike into the desert near Carajo, Arizona, and spend a week picking the brain of a Retired Thunderbird. Where *he* gets *his* ideas, I have no idea whatsoever." But the thunderbird tale is merely a fable to protect the privacy of his formidably successful creative process.

The fact is that Seuss, born in Springfield, Massachusetts, in 1904, has been doodling cartoon characters strongly reminiscent of his famous menagerie since his student days at Dartmouth and Oxford. He still has an Oxford notebook containing images similar to those in the famous *Cat in the Hat*, the book he published to wide acclaim in 1950. From hatted cat to hated grinch, the familiar creatures have prowled his imagination for much of the century. □

Theodor S. Geisel, better known as Dr. Seuss, relaxes in his La Jolla, California, study above the Pacific.

Mental Mutt

Winston Churchill, Britain's great wartime prime minister, suffered from lifelong fits of depression—the Black Dog, as he called it. Paradoxically, this same creature of the mind may have spurred the restless creative energy, combative fire, and infectious courage that made Churchill the architect of his nation's finest hour.

The grandson of a duke, Churchill grew up a frail and neglected child who forced himself to become fearless and physically tough through sheer will.

Even by the aloof standards of the Edwardian era, Churchill's aristocratic parents ignored him.

For parental warmth, he substituted enormous ambition. "We are all worms," he said. "But I do believe that I am a glow-worm."

Psychological analysts have argued that an emotionally deprived child who later falls victim to depression suffers from difficulty in disposing of hostility. At bad moments, Churchill's hostility turned inward, leaving him convinced of his worthlessness. But, faced with a real target in Adolf Hitler, whose menace Churchill sensed so early, he was able to tap wellsprings of heroic defiance.

Like many other depressives, Churchill was driven to ceaseless activity to keep his personal demons at bay. "Winston has always

Winston Churchill often kept his melancholia at bay by painting, as in this 1946 interlude at a Swiss villa on the shores of Lake Geneva.

been wretched unless occupied," a colleague once observed. Restlessness helped fuel his prolific writing and led him to take up the hobby of painting to dispel a depressive bout.

Sadly, his Black Dog won in the end. Nothing could fend off Churchill's depression after 1955, when he retired from the public life that had been his creative theater. Before he died at ninety-one, in 1965, he endured long years wrapped in suffocating gloom. □

Ear Trouble

Vincent van Gogh has long epitomized the mentally tortured artist. His peculiar blend of genius and madness has become a kind of shorthand explanation for the jarring intensity and nonconformity of his work—a lifetime output of 800 oil paintings and 700 drawings, all indelibly marked with the artist's increasingly tormented personality. The sad details of the Dutch impressionist's personal life have reinforced his madman's image: his lonely, penniless existence; his slashing off of part of his left ear in 1888 as a gory gift for a prostitute; his 1889 decision to commit himself to an asylum for epileptics; and finally, his suicide in 1890 at the age of thirty-seven.

For many scholars, it has not been enough to say merely that van Gogh was brilliant but mentally unstable. The real causes of his instability have become for many an enduring mystery and a perennial source for medical speculation. The latest diagnosis is dramatic in its simplicity: Van Gogh may have suffered not from some terrible deterioration of the mind, but of the ear—a malady known as Ménière's syndrome, caused by excess fluid and pressure in the inner ear.

I. Kaufman Arenberg of the Swedish Medical Center in Englewood, Colorado, has advanced this thesis after studying 796 letters that van Gogh wrote between 1884 and 1890, the years of his most intense productivity in oil painting. In the correspondence, van Gogh wrote friends of hearing strange sounds and of suffering vertigo for days, then of spending months without such symptoms. Those are common signs of Ménière's syndrome, according to Arenberg, who invented a surgical valve to treat the disease. Ménière's, which was first described in 1861 but rarely diagnosed until the twentieth century, affects hearing and balance and causes nausea, deafness, and ringing in the ears. More than seven million Americans may be afflicted, and thousands of patients have described their symptoms much as van Gogh did his own.

The Ménière's thesis supplants a view that van Gogh may have suffered from temporal lobe epilepsy, which can also produce distorted vision, fits of hyper-religiosity, and periodic aggressiveness—all symptoms that van Gogh exhibited. Earlier, experts thought he may have suffered from glaucoma or digitalis poisoning, both of which cause distorted vision, or addiction to absinthe or turpentine, which causes brain deterioration.

But none of the explanations lays bare the essential mystery: It was not while manic, but in a state of deep depression in the late 1870s that van Gogh first decided to draw. And some inner discipline of the creative mind permitted him to transcend his illness, whatever its nature, to change art forever. □

Vincent van Gogh painted this self-portrait after slicing off his earlobe in a fit of rage.

Lewis in Wonderland

A creative surge is sometimes called a brainstorm, a term that also describes the violent electro-chemical tempests known as epilepsy *(page 19)*. In the view of some modern researchers, the double meaning exactly describes the mind of Charles Lutwidge Dodgson, also known as Lewis Carroll.

As Dodgson, Carroll was an Oxford University mathematician and logician, who dreamed up *Alice's Adventures in Wonderland* and *Through the Looking Glass* to amuse the children of an academic colleague. Carroll had a bad stammer and spoke much more easily to children than adults. He also suffered from severe migraine headaches, which, along with pain, sometimes cause auras and blank spots in the sufferer's vision.

In Carroll's stories, Alice shares some of those characteristics in the course of her adventures. Her growing, shrinking, and neck-stretching resemble the changes in the size of objects in a migraine victim's vision. In *Through the Looking Glass*, Alice looks in vain for a fleeting bright object that present-day scholars find reminiscent of a migraine aura.

Experts now believe that Carroll's symptoms might also have indicated temporal lobe epilepsy, a form of the disorder that can be accompanied by hypergraphia, a strange impulse to write detailed letters, diaries, and other works. This form of epilepsy can also involve auditory and visual hallucinations and feelings of being outside one's body—conditions familiar to Alice, and, it appears, to Lewis Carroll himself. □

An illness may have led author Lewis Carroll to imagine size aberrations for his characters, such as the stretching of Alice's neck on her first journey to Wonderland, depicted in the famous Sir John Tenniel illustration.

Dialogue with Death

Arthur Koestler, the Hungarian-born novelist and philosopher, thought deeply about the sources of creation. In his book *The Art of Creativity*, he developed the theory of what he called bisociation, which argues that new ideas depend on the unconscious combining of ideas that the conscious mind normally considers to be incompatible. But the creative themes that he developed in his own fiction were derived from something very different: a long period of solitary confinement under the threat of death.

Koestler, for years a secret German Communist Party member, posed as an independent journalist during the Spanish Civil War. In 1937, he was unmasked and arrested by the Spanish fascists as a spy. He spent the next three months in a Seville jail, where, every night, he heard firing squads execute his fellow prisoners. With each volley, he wondered if he would be next. So intense was the experience that he came to see death as an actual person, who "tripped down the corridor" and "danced pirouettes."

Much of the time he spent entirely alone, under conditions that stripped away his intellectual defenses. Eventually, he later observed, "my brain was drained dry and the few drops of thought that I squeezed out of it were pale, like thrice-brewed tea." The dreadful process of being leached of intellectual activity finally drove him inward to think "only about absolutes and very basic, fundamental problems." Koestler thereby achieved a new kind of "oceanic" insight, a "spiritual transformation" that eroded his previous "rational, materialistic way of thinking." Among other things, his new insights led him to cast aside his doctrinaire Marxist view of man as a purely economic animal and replace it with a more mystical view of the human being as a spiritual creature, with both infinite and finite dimensions of being.

Eventually, an international campaign led to Koestler's release. One of his first acts was to memorialize his prison experiences in *Dialogue with Death*, part of his three-volume autobiography. The conflict between spiritualism and the relentless materialism of totalitarian thinking that he discovered in those awful prison months became the basis of many of his finest novels, including his masterpiece, *Darkness at Noon*.

Decades after his imprisonment, Koestler met with a British journalist, Anthony Grey, who had spent months alone under house arrest during the Chinese Cultural Revolution of 1966. The two men agreed that the intense loneliness they had experienced gave them insights into the human condition—and the creative recesses of their own minds—that were simply unavailable at any lower price. □

Hungarian writer Arthur Koestler, shown in Paris in 1946, the year that French translations of his *Darkness at Noon* sparked a national debate on communist principles.

Close Czech

The world that Franz Kafka created in his writings is arbitrary and terrifying. A man wakes up transformed into a giant insect. A prisoner dies as his sentence is carved into his back by an engine of torture. A man is tried and sentenced without discovering what crime he has committed. More than any other modern writer, the Czech-born Kafka, who died of tuberculosis in 1924 at age forty, captured the plight of hapless, alienated individuals in a bureaucratic age.

It now appears, however, that Kafka was not simply inventing a frightening world. Instead, he mirrored one that was as real and terrifying as the nightmares he invented. Creativity was his private defense against insanity.

From all accounts, Kafka suffered from profound identity problems induced by his father, a boorish, domineering Prague merchant. The son never broke free of that blighting influence, which left him feeling profoundly guilty, fearful, and unsure of himself. "I am nothing but a mass of spikes going through me," he wrote.

He was subject to near-psychotic fantasies: Writing to a friend about mice in his bedroom, he told of fears that they had "riddled the surrounding walls through and through with their tunnels, and are lurking within."

Most people who feel powerless in the outside world create inner realms that they can control. Kafka retreated into his writing, the only activity that gave him a strong sense of self. "I have no literary interest, but am made of literature," he wrote. "I am nothing else, and cannot be anything else."

At the same time, Kafka knew that his creative cocoon was no substitute for a more assertive, normal life. He expressed the paradox of personal insecurity in "The Burrow," a harrowing tale of a nameless animal that builds an elaborate honeycomb of passages underground, where he can sleep "the sweet sleep of tranquillity, of satisfied desire, of achieved ambition." The animal occasionally steals outside, ignoring the risk to gloat over his secret place from a distance. But the beast is still insecure. What, he wonders, if someone finds the entrance to his lair?

Before his premature death, Kafka had achieved enough success to gain some self-confidence. Like his burrowing creature, he took pride in the literary edifice he had created, in spite of—or because of—his terrible inner fears. □

Franz Kafka poses diffidently during the 1920s in front of his home in Prague, where he spent much of his tormented life.

Man in Block

The mind now and then decides to stop the flow of creative energy that causes the poet to lift his pen or the novelist to turn to her typewriter. This damming of the stream produces symptoms that, in writing at least, are called writer's block. When it occurs, it seems to destroy the bridge between the writer and the written word, causing productivity to dry up, sometimes forever. But writer's block may carry benefits as well.

Rainer Maria Rilke, one of the foremost lyric poets of the twentieth century, offers a curious case in point. Born in Prague in 1875 and educated there, Rilke moved to Germany and traveled to Russia on a trip that helped inspire his work. In the early 1900s, he created an entirely new form of German lyric poetry, which he called the object poem. It tried to capture the essence of a subject in words the way that painters and sculptors did in oils or clay. In 1910, Rilke transformed the German prose landscape with *Notebook of Malte Laurids Brigge*, a study of the "disintegration of the soul."

Soon after, Rilke fell into a deep depression. His powers failed. Suspended helplessly in a colossal writer's block, he published nothing for thirteen years. For a decade of that time, he wrote only two of the so-called Duino elegies, named for a stay at Duino Castle, near Trieste, Italy. Rilke considered giving up writing entirely.

In the summer of 1921, however, he moved to the Château de Muzot in Switzerland's Rhone Valley. The following February, the oppressive block suddenly lifted, and Rilke began to work ceaselessly. In eighteen days, he finished the Duino cycle and produced another fifty-five linked poems, *Sonnets to Orpheus*. These are considered his greatest works. In all, he wrote 1,200 lines of exquisite poetry, largely without correction. The block never returned, and Rilke continued to produce, though less spectacularly, until his death in 1926 from leukemia.

No one knows what caused his monumental block or why it lifted when it did. But it may be that, in some cryptic fashion, his mind arranged the lengthy drought to prepare for the intense literary flood that it knew must follow. □

Duino Castle *(above)* **inspired some of the best work of German poet Rainer Maria Rilke** *(foreground)*, **once a victim of extreme writer's block.**

Potent Pixies

While the ancient Greeks invoked the Muses for inspiration, the nineteenth-century Scottish novelist Robert Louis Stevenson relied on what he dubbed Brownies. That was the puckish name Stevenson, the author of *Treasure Island* and *Kidnapped,* gave to the mysterious alchemy that worked in his mind at night, doing "one-half my work for me while I am fast asleep." When his creativity dried up, Stevenson would often simply close his eyes to the problem. Then, he claimed, his "sleepless Brownies" would give him "better tales than he could fashion for himself."

The writer specifically credited his nocturnal elves with furnishing the plot ingredients for *The Strange Case of Dr. Jekyll and Mr. Hyde.* "For two days," he wrote, "I went about racking my brains for a plot of any sort" for a story of "man's double being." Then he had two dreams—one involving the transformation of the benign Jekyll into the evil Hyde, and another in which Hyde, who was being pursued for some crime, turned back into peaceable Dr. Jekyll in front of his pursuers. Stevenson devised the rest of the tale while awake.

Stevenson's Brownies—as he himself was keenly aware—were his creative unconscious, a dark place in the mind from which his art arose. It had not always worked so well for him, however. When he was a child, this same mental domain produced nightmares that made him wake up screaming. As Stevenson grew older, the dreams lost some of their power, but he still awoke now and then with "a flying heart, a freezing scalp, cold sweats, and the speechless midnight fear." As a student at Edinburgh University, Stevenson sought the help of doctors to ease the burden. The treatment evidently worked. When he became a professional writer, Stevenson liked to relate, his house-trained horrors helped, rather than hindered, his literary labors. □

A horrified Dr. Lanyon looks on as the evil Mr. Hyde drinks a steaming potion and is transformed back into gentle Dr. Henry Jekyll, in Robert Louis Stevenson's dream-inspired tale.

Satanic Strains

Many innovators have claimed divine inspiration for their work. But Giuseppe Tartini, a renowned eighteenth-century Italian composer, violinist, and music teacher, gave his own twist to the custom: The source for his best composition, he claimed, was Satan.

Born into a titled family in 1692, Tartini supposedly encountered Lucifer while hiding at the monastery of Assisi. He had fled there to escape a powerful cardinal's rage after eloping with one of the churchman's protégés. Tartini was already an accomplished musician and innovator when he arrived at Assisi, and he spent some of his nearly two years there redesigning the violin bow and composing.

As Tartini later told friends,

he dreamed one night that he had made a Faustian bargain with Satan: his soul in exchange for a variety of wishes. On impulse, Tartini had handed Lucifer his violin. "Great was my astonishment when I heard him play, with consummate skill, a sonata of such exquisite beauty as surpassed the boldest flights of my imagination," Tartini recounted. "I felt enraptured, transported, enchanted; my

breath failed me, and—I awoke."

Rushing to his violin, Tartini attempted to reproduce the beautiful satanic strains—and failed. He then composed music that he said was the best he ever wrote, and yet, "How far was it beneath the one I had heard in my dream!" Giving credit where it was due, Tartini called the sonata that he had salvaged *Trillo del Diavolo:* the Devil's Trill. □

Survival Instincts

Great minds think alike less often than the old adage implies. But every so often an important idea seems to rise spontaneously in several imaginations—especially in the realm of science.

One of the most famous cases of such conceptual convergence involved Charles Darwin *(far right),* author of *Origin of Species,* and Alfred Russell Wallace *(right),* a self-taught botanist and insect collector. Both had the same profound insight, that species evolve in their environments by natural selection—survival of the fittest.

The cautious and methodical Darwin had elaborated much of his

idea by 1842, six years after the famed five-year voyage of HMS *Beagle.* However, he held back his findings while he worked on other elements of evolution. Wallace, on the other hand, conceived the main elements of evolutionary theory in a two-hour bout of inspiration in the Malay Archipelago and fired them off to Darwin in 1858 in a twenty-page letter. Chagrined, Darwin pushed forward with his contro-

versial magnum opus a year later. But in the meantime, the two naturalists had unveiled their findings jointly—even though they had come upon the same idea sixteen years apart. □

Enclaves

Although the creative mind works mostly alone, it has a gregarious side too, a strong urge to clump with others in kindred concentrations. This may be for stimulation, reinforcement, or defense against an unsupportive community; like so much else about creativity, the cause is less obvious than the effect.

A dramatic example of the intellectual herd instinct in this century was the flocking of American artists of all kinds to Paris after both world wars—in the 1920s and the 1950s. In the period from 1918 to 1932, it seemed that all of America's literary lights drank coffee and visited salons on the Parisian Left Bank. Among the great names were Ezra Pound, Ernest Hemingway, F. Scott Fitzgerald, e. e. cummings, John Dos Passos, William Carlos Williams, William Faulkner, Katherine Anne Porter, Henry Miller, and James Thurber. "There are no problems," Ernest Hemingway wrote of Paris, "except where to be happiest."

One reason for the unusual concentration of Americans in France was an inhospitable climate at home. In the wake of World War I, the United States had grown introspective and puritanical. Paris, a haven for intellectual exiles since the French Revolution, was tolerant of foreigners, cosmopolitan, and cheap, and for blacks it was also less racist than the United States.

But the tendency of intellectuals, writers, and artists to gravitate together is more a behavioral characteristic than a taste for France. All over the world, similar concentrations of talent can be found. London's raffish Soho district has long been a magnet.

With astonishing speed, the area of small factories and businesses south of Houston Street in Manhattan—therefore called SoHo—became another. In the space of two decades, New York's SoHo, with its more than 150 art galleries and innumerable studios, ousted Greenwich Village as the city's main artistic haven, a role the Village had occupied for more than a century. SoHo has now become too expensive for struggling intellectual talent, some of which is pioneering in New Jersey.

The Yugoslavian region of Slovenia boasts the iconoclastic Slowenische Kunst, an art collective with everything from a rock group, to artists and architects, to a theater troupe called Red Pilot. Almost a contradiction in terms, its creative people are staunchly anonymous.

Taos and Santa Fe, New Mexico, are noted havens for artists and craftspeople, building on the creative legacies of the previous landowners, the Navajo. Florida's Key West has drawn talented Americans since the days of James Audubon, the painter and naturalist. Less

well-known is the congeries of creativity at the Hunter's Point Naval Shipyard in San Francisco, where the navy sublets space to 300 artists, and in Haines, Alaska, a fishing village that became an artists' colony in 1947 when an army post sublet its housing. In Haines, another attraction was the chance to revive the previously resident Tlingit Indian craft culture.

In addition to spontaneous congregations, there are some thirty officially consecrated artists' colonies around the United States, most of them offering havens to creative spirits for limited periods. Their aim is usually to support specific creative endeavors, and some, such as the MacDowell Colony in Peterborough, New Hampshire, go to great lengths to free up creative time for guests, even delivering meals to studio doors.

Still, France draws more than its share of creative spirits, drawn not only to Paris, but to other centers as well. One notable example: Château de La Garenne-Lemot, a 200-year-old Loire Valley estate recently converted into a collection of artists' studios. La Garenne-Lemot evokes the old days in France, except that it boasts more than a wave of expatriate Americans: Its artists come from everywhere, including Russia—and even France. □

Golden Ages

Just as brilliant individuals stand out from their fellows, some times and places give off a special glow of intense creativity. Athens in the fifth century BC, Elizabethan England and the sixteenth-century Netherlands, China during the Ming dynasty 350 years ago, Paris in the Enlightenment and again before and after World War I, Berlin in the 1920s—each venue seems to have been especially endowed with genius and creative fertility.

While such creative eras are universally recognized, their sources remain obscure. Often they seem poised between times of great change and those of excessive stability. For example, the most creative period in Egyptian history—beginning in about 2700 BC—started with the consolidation of the unitary state, the spread of

irrigation, and the development of agricultural methods that would feed a large work force. But within the space of a century, the same unitary state became a deadening hand on creativity that froze forms of cultural expression for hundreds of years.

Elizabethan England emerged from a time of civil strife; the explosion of modern art in Europe paralleled the rise of revolutionary socialism in Russia. One fact seems unarguable: Where cultural creativity is encouraged, as in Renaissance Florence, it grows; where it is suppressed, as in Stalinist Russia, it retreats.

But no matter what the cultural conditions, human creativity cannot sustain its highest pitch indefinitely. Thus, what seem to be fallow periods between richly creative eras may only be naps that renew the creative spirit. □

ACKNOWLEDGMENTS

The editors wish to thank these individuals and institutions for their valuable assistance in the preparation of this volume:

Alamoudi Abdurahman, Muslim American Council, Washington, D.C.; Dina Abramowicz, YIVO Institute for Jewish Research, New York; David G. Amaral, The Salk Institute, San Diego, California; Derek Bickerton, Department of Linguistics, University of Hawaii, Honolulu; Alan Bombard, Bandol, France; James Byrnes, University of Maryland, College Park; Michael Deakin, London; William Diver, Columbia University, New York; Giorgio Dragoni, Dipartimento di Fisica, Università di Bologna, Bologna; Sybille Duelli, Ullstein Langen-Müller Verlag, Berlin; Robert Eisen, Department of Religious Studies, George Washington University, Washington, D.C.; Irene Elce, Penfield Archive, McIntyre Medical Sciences Building, Montreal; Dietrich von Engelhardt, Institut für Medizin-und Wissenschaftsgeschichte, Medical Universität, Lübeck, Germany; Franco Ferraroti, Università degli Studi, Rome; Doug Fizel, American Psychological Association, Public Affairs, Washington, D.C.; Frank Halpern, Free Library of Philadelphia; Carolyn Heveran, Lee Strasberg Theatre Institute, New York; Istituto Archeologico Germanico, Rome; John A. Jager, Alzheimer's Association, New York; Marcel Kinsbourne, Winchester, Massachusetts; George Koltanowski, San Francisco; John Larson, Bonney Center, University of California, Irvine; Elizabeth Loftus, University of Washington, Seattle; Charles J. Lumsden, Medical Sciences Building, University of Toronto, Toronto; Dan Mahony, Ipswich, Massachusetts; Franca Principe, Istituto e Museo di Storia della Scienza, Florence; Christopher Rawlings, British Library, London; Christine Ritter, Vienna; Dennis Sacuzzo, San Diego State University, San Diego, California; Jimmy Neil Smith, National Association for the Preservation and Perpetuation of Storytelling, Jonesboro, Tennessee; Elizabeth Stapleton, Royal Earlswood, Redhill, Surrey; William C. Stokoe, Emeritus of Gallaudet College, Silver Spring, Maryland; Ertel Suitbert, Institut für Psychologie, Göttingen, Germany; Shinichi Suzuki, Talent Education Institute, Matsumoto City, Nagano Prefecture, Japan; Henry Sweets, The Mark Twain Museum, Hannibal, Missouri; David Tumey, Dayton, Ohio; Rosalyn Tureck, New York; Sandra F. Witelson, Department of Psychiatry, McMaster University, Hamilton, Ontario.

PICTURE CREDITS

The sources for the illustrations that appear in this book are listed below. Credits from left to right are separated by semicolons; from top to bottom by dashes.

Cover: © Lennart Nilsson, *The Incredible Machine,* National Geographic Society, Washington, D.C., background, Biophoto Associates/Science Source/Photo Researchers, Inc., New York. **3:** © Lennart Nilsson, *The Incredible Machine,* National Geographic Society, Washington, D.C. **7:** David Spindel/Superstock, New York, background, CNRI/SPL/Science Source/Photo Researchers, Inc., New York. **8:** Roger-Viollet, Paris. **9:** Giraudon, Paris; Jean-Loup Charmet, Paris—courtesy The Ferdinand Hamburger, Jr. Archives of The Johns Hopkins University, Baltimore. **10, 11:** David Spindel/Superstock, New York. **12:** Marcus E. Raichle. **13:** Marcus E. Raichle; Lauros/Giraudon/ADAGP, courtesy Musée de la Ville de Paris, Musée Bourdelle; Bulloz, Paris, courtesy Musée Victor Hugo. **15:** CNRI/SPL/Science Source/Photo Researchers, Inc., New York. **16, 17:** Dr. C. Chumbley/Science Source/Photo Researchers, Inc., New York. **18:** Giancarlo Costa, Milan. **20:** From *A Textbook of Epilepsy,* by John Laidlaw et al., third edition, published by Churchill Livingstone, Edinburgh, 1988. **21:** Jeffrey Rycus. **22:** © Lennart Nilsson, *The Incredible Machine,* National Geographic Society, Washington, D.C. **23:** Photo by Walter Salinger, courtesy of Anthony DeCasper; Renée Comet, copied from *The Cat in the Hat,* by Dr. Seuss, © 1957 by Dr. Seuss, copyright renewed 1986 by Theodor S. Geisel & Audrey S. Geisel, reprinted by permission of Random House, Inc., New York. **24, 25:** E. Mandelman/World Health Organization, Geneva; Michael Lewis, from *Shame: The Exposed Self,* Free Press, 1991. **26:** Courtesy Roger Morgan. **27:** Jacqueline Duvoisin/*Sports Illustrated.* **28:** Library of Congress LC62-93205. **29:** Cordon Art, Amsterdam. **31:** Art by Time-Life Books. **32, 33:** Collection of Albert Kahn-Department des Hauts de Seine. **35:** Chuck Fishman © 1983/Woodfin Camp & Associates, Washington, D.C. **36:** Courtesy Paul D. MacLean, *Journal of Nervous and Mental Disease,* 1967. **39:** © 1990 Louis Psihoyos/Matrix, New York, background, Michael Stuckey/Comstock, New York. **40:** By permission of Harvard University Archives, Cambridge, Massachusetts. **41:** Mark Sexton, courtesy Dr. Elliot Sagall, Boston. **42:** Bildarchiv Preussischer Kulturbesitz, Berlin. **43:** Syndication International, London. **44:** E. F. Clark, Bedford, England. **45:** AP/Wide World Photos, New York. **46:** C. M. Frank. **47:** Mrs. Margaret Mott, Edinburgh. **48:** Stichting Nederlands Foto & Grafisch Centrum—Barton Silverman/NYT Pictures, New York. **49:** Sal Di Marco. **50:** © 1990 Louis Psihoyos/Matrix, New York. **51:** Masachika Suhara/© Discover Publications Inc., New York. **52:** Originally appeared in *Omni* magazine, July 1981, courtesy of American Mensa Ltd., Brooklyn, New York. **53:** Vicki Lewis, Washington, D.C. **54:** Dr. John Lorber, Tewkesbury, Gloucestershire. **55:** © *Christian Science Monitor* by Daniel Wood, Boston. **56:** Sovfoto, New York. **57:** Talent Education Institute, Nagano, Japan. **58, 59:** Jim Coit, San Diego, California, courtesy The Repository for Germinal Choice, Escondido, California; Ray Jerome Baker, Bishop Museum, Honolulu; photo by G. de Srebnickioi, courtesy of Mijanou Bourdelon. **60:** G. K. and Vicki Hart/The Image Bank, New York. **61:** Jerry Jacka Photography, Phoenix. **62:** Erich Lessing/Kunsthistorisches Museum, Vienna. **63:** Renée Comet, Washington, D.C. **65:** From *Mental Deficiency,* by A. F. Tredgold, published by Baillière, Tindall & Cox, London, 1908. **67:** © copyrighted, Chicago Tribune Company/Michael Fryer. **68:** Bill Epridge for *Life.* **69:** Ray Ng, Denver. **70:** Michael Abramson/Sipa Press, New York. **71:** Paul Meredith for *Life.* **73:** Salvador Dali, *The Persistence of Memory,* 1931, collection, The Museum of Modern Art, New York, background, Craig Aurness/Westlight, Los Angeles. **74:** Alinari/Art Resource, New York; courtesy Archives of the History of American Psychology, University of Akron, Akron, Ohio. **75:** Renée Comet, Washington, D.C. **76:** Courtesy of the Literary Executors of the Penfield Archive, Montreal Neurological Institute and McGill University, Montreal. **77:** Art by Time-Life Books. **78:** Courtesy The Lee Strasberg Theatre Institute, New York. **79:** Courtesy Mary Carter Smith. **80:** © 1987 George Steinmetz. **81:** AP/Wide World Photos, New York. **82:** The Bettmann Archive, New York. **83:** Judy Manzelman—courtesy Prints & Photo Division, History of Medicine Division, National Library of Medicine, Bethesda, Maryland. **84:** The Bettmann Archive, New York. **85:** Photo by Kerry Herman, courtesy WNET, New York. **86:** From *Cognition,* by M. W. Matlin, Holt, Rinehart & Winston, New York, 1989. **87:** The Image Bank, New York. **88:** From *Cognition,* by M. W. Matlin, Holt, Rinehart & Winston, New York, 1989. **89:** Photo by John Gregory, courtesy Santelli, Englewood, New Jersey—Renée Comet, Washington, D.C. **90:** Renée Comet, Washington, D.C. **91:** AP/Wide World Photos, New York. **92:** From *Foundations of Cyclopean Perception,* by Bela Julesz, The University of Chicago Press, Chicago, 1971. **93:** Bibliothèque Nationale, Paris. **94:** Library of Congress LC-104498—Peter Johansky/FPG, New York. **95:** The Hulton Picture Company, London. **96:** Robert Hupka. **97:** Art by Time-Life Books. **98, 99:** From *Food & Drink: A Pictorial Archive from Nineteenth Century Sources,* Dover Publications, Inc., New York, 1980; Renée Comet, Washington, D.C. **100:** *Washington Post* photo

BIBLIOGRAPHY

Books

Ali, Maulana Muhammad. *The Holy Qur'ān: Arabic Text, English Translation and Commentary* (6th ed., rev.). Lahore, Pakistan: Ahmadiyyah Anjuman Isha'at Islam, 1973.

Bartlett, Frederic C. *Remembering: A Study in Experimental and Social Psychology.* Cambridge: Cambridge University Press, 1977 (reprint of 1932 edition).

Benderly, Beryl Lieff. *The Myth of Two Minds: What Gender Means and Doesn't Mean.* New York: Doubleday, 1987.

Bergland, Richard. *The Fabric of Mind.* New York: Viking, 1985.

Blakemore, Colin, and Susan Greenfield (Eds.). *Mindwaves: Thoughts on Intelligence, Identity and Consciousness.* Oxford: Basil Blackwell, 1987.

Blanchard, Edward B., and Leonard H. Epstein. *A Biofeedback Primer.* Reading, Mass.: Addison-Wesley, 1978.

Bolles, Edmund Blair. *Remembering and Forgetting: An Inquiry into the Nature of Memory.* New York: Walker, 1988.

The Brain: A User's Manual. New York: G. P. Putnam's Sons, Perigee Books, 1987.

Brockett, Oscar G. *History of the Theatre* (3rd ed.). Boston: Allyn & Bacon, 1978.

Burt, Cyril. *The Gifted Child.* New York: John Wiley & Sons, Halsted Press Book, 1975.

Campos, Joseph J., et al. "Socioemotional Development." *Infancy and Developmental Psychobiology,* edited by Marshall M. Haith and Joseph J. Campos (Vol. 2 of *Handbook of Child Psychology* (4th ed.), edited by Paul H. Mussen). New York: John Wiley & Sons, 1983.

Carlson, Neil R. *Physiology of Behavior.* Boston: Allyn & Bacon, 1981.

Chukovsky, Kornei. *From Two to Five.* Translated and edited by Miriam Morton. Berkeley: University of California Press, 1971.

Clark, E. F. *George Parker Bidder: The Calculating Boy.* Bedford, England: KSL, 1983.

Cohen, Daniel. *Creativity: What Is It?* New York: M. Evans, 1977.

Colles, H. C. *New Grove: Dictionary of Music and Musicians* (3rd ed.). New York: Macmillan, 1939.

Corliss, William R. (Comp.). *Strange Minds: A Sourcebook of Unusual Mental Phenomena* (Vol. P-1). Glen Arm, Md.: Sourcebook Project, 1976.

Einstein, Alfred. *Mozart: His Character, His Work.* Translated by Arthur Mendel and Nathan Broder. London: Oxford University Press, 1945.

Escher, M. C. *Escher on Escher: Exploring the Infinite.* Translated by Karin Ford. New York: Harry N. Abrams, 1989.

Feldman, David Henry, and Lynn T. Goldsmith. *Nature's Gambit: Child Prodigies and the Development of Human Potential.* New York: Basic Books, 1986.

Feldman, Ruth Duskin. *Whatever Happened to the Quiz Kids? Perils and Profits of Growing Up Gifted.* Chicago: Chicago Review Press, 1982.

Frankl, Viktor E. *Man's Search for Meaning: An Introduction to Logotherapy* (3rd ed., rev.). Translated by Ilse Lasch. New York: Simon & Schuster, Touchstone Book, 1984.

Gardner, Howard. *Art, Mind, and Brain: A Cognitive Approach to Creativity.* New York: Basic Books, 1982.

Garfield, Charles A., and Hal Zina Bennett. *Peak Performance: Mental Training Techniques of the World's Greatest Athletes.* Los Angeles: Jeremy P. Tarcher, 1984.

Ghiselin, Brewster. *The Creative Process: A Symposium.* Berkeley: University of California Press, 1952.

Gillispie, Charles Coulston (Ed.). *Dictionary of Scientific Biography* (Vol. 4). New York: Charles Scribner's Sons, 1971.

Gregory, Richard L. (Ed.). *The Oxford Companion to the Mind.* London: Oxford University Press, 1987.

Gruber, Howard E. *Darwin on Man: A Psychological Study of Scientific Creativity* (2nd ed.). Chicago: University of Chicago Press, 1981.

Guinness Book of World Records 1989. New York: Sterling, 1988.

Guinness Book of World Records 1990. New York: Sterling, 1989.

Hadamard, Jacques. *The Psychology of Invention in the Mathematical Field.* New Jersey: Princeton University Press, 1945.

Hagen, Uta, and Haskel Frankel. *Respect for Acting.* New York: Macmillan, 1973.

Hamilton, Iain. *Koestler: A Biography.* New York: Macmillan, 1982.

Harding, Rosamond E. M. *An Anatomy of Inspiration: And an Essay on the Creative Mood.* Cambridge: W. Heffer & Sons, 1948.

Harris, P. L. "Infant Cognition." *Infancy and Developmental Psychobiology,* edited by Marshall M. Haith and Joseph J. Campos (Vol. 2 of *Handbook of Child Psychology* (4th ed.), edited by Paul H. Mussen). New York: John Wiley & Sons, 1983.

Herrigel, Eugen. *Zen: In the Art of Archery.* Translated by R. F. C. Hull. New York: Vintage Books, 1971.

Hilgard, Ernest R. *Divided Consciousness: Multiple Controls in Human Thought and Action.* New York: John Wiley & Sons, 1977.

Ho, Wai-Ching (Ed.). *Yani: The Brush of Innocence.* New York: Hudson Hills Press; Kansas City: Nelson-Atkins Museum of Art, 1989.

Hooper, Judith, and Dick Teresi. *The Three-Pound Universe.* New York: Macmillan, 1986.

Jensen, Arthur R. *Straight Talk about Mental Tests.* New York: Macmillan, Free Press, 1981.

Kamin, Leon J. *The Science and Politics of I.Q.* Potomac, Md.: Lawrence Erlbaum Associates; New York: John Wiley & Sons, 1974.

Kinsbourne, Marcel, and Merrill Hiscock. "The Normal and Deviant Development of Functional Lateralization of the Brain." *Infancy and Developmental Psychobiology,* edited by Marshall M. Haith and Joseph J. Campos (Vol. 2 of *Handbook of Child Psychology* (4th ed.), edited by Paul H. Mussen). New York: John Wiley & Sons, 1983.

Klima, Edward S., et al. *The Signs of Language.* Cambridge: Harvard University Press, 1979.

Koestler, Arthur:
Darkness at Noon. Translated by Daphne Hardy. New York: Macmillan, 1952.
Dialogue with Death. Translated by Trevor Blewitt and Phyllis Blewitt. New York: Macmillan, 1942.

Koltanowski, George. *Adventures of a Chess Master.* Edited by Milton Finkelstein. New York: David McKay, 1955.

Lash, Joseph P. *Helen and Teacher: The Story of Helen Keller and Anne Sullivan* (Radcliffe Biography series). New York: Delacorte Press/Seymour Lawrence, Merloyd Lawrence Book, 1980.

Loftus, Geoffrey R., and Elizabeth F. Loftus. *Human Memory: The Processing of Information.* Hillsdale, N.J.: Lawrence Erlbaum Associates, 1976.

Luria, A. R. *The Mind of a Mnemonist.* Translated by Lynn Solotaroff. New York: Basic Books, 1968.

MacLean, Paul D. *The Triune Brain in Evolution: Role in Paleocerebral Functions.* New York: Plenum Press, 1990.

McLeish, Kenneth. *Children of the Gods.* England: Harlow, Essex & Longman, 1983.

Madigan, Carol Orsag, and Ann Elwood. *Brainstorms & Thunderbolts: How Creative Genius Works.* New York: Macmillan, 1983.

Maps of the Mind. New York: Macmillan, 1981.

Marek, George R. *Toscanini.* New York: Atheneum, 1975.

Matlin, M. W. *Cognition* (2nd ed.). New York: Holt, Rinehart & Winston, 1989.

Neppe, Vernon M. *The Psychology of Déjà Vu: Have I Been Here Before?* Johannesburg: Witwatersrand University Press, 1983.

Nicklaus, Jack, and Ken Bowden. *Golf My Way.* New York: Simon & Schuster, 1974.

Norman, Donald A. *Memory and Attention: An Introduction to Human Information Processing.* New York: John Wiley & Sons, 1969.

Obler, Loraine K., and Deborah Fein (Eds.). *The Exceptional Brain: Neuropsychology of Talent and Special Abilities.* New York: Guilford Press, 1988.

Osborn, Alex. *Your Creative Power: How to Use Imagination.* New York: Charles Scribner's Sons, 1952.

Packard, Vance. *The Hidden Persuaders* (rev. ed.). New York: Pocket Books, Washington Square Press, 1980.

Paine, Albert Bigelow:
The Boys' Life of Mark Twain. Edited by Walter Barnes. New York: Harper & Brothers, 1929.
Mark Twain (Vol. 2) (American Men and Women of Letters series). Edited by Daniel Aaron.

New York: Chelsea House, 1980.

Penfield, Wilder. *The Mystery of the Mind: A Critical Study of Consciousness and the Human Brain.* Princeton, N.J.: Princeton University Press, 1975.

Perkins, D. N. *The Mind's Best Work.* Cambridge, Mass.: Harvard University Press, 1981.

Prescott, F. C. (Ed.). *Selections from the Critical Writings of Edgar Allan Poe.* New York: Gordian Press, 1981.

Psychology Today: An Introduction (5th ed.). New York: Random House, 1975.

Radford, John. *Child Prodigies and Exceptional Early Achievers.* New York: Macmillan, Free Press, 1990.

Restak, Richard M.:
The Brain. New York: Bantam Books, 1984.
The Infant Mind. Garden City, N.Y.: Doubleday, 1986.
The Mind. New York: Bantam Books, 1988.

Rose, Steven. *The Conscious Brain* (rev. ed.). New York: Paragon House, 1989.

Rosenfield, Israel. *The Invention of Memory: A New View of the Brain.* New York: Basic Books, 1988.

Rosner, Stanley, and Lawrence E. Abt (Eds.). *The Creative Experience.* New York: Grossman, 1970.

Sacchi, Filippo. *The Magic Baton: Toscanini's Life for Music.* New York: G. P. Putnam's Sons, 1957.

Saccuzzo, Dennis P. *Psychology: From Research to Applications.* Newton, Mass.: Allyn & Bacon, 1987.

Sacks, Oliver. *The Man Who Mistook His Wife for a Hat: And Other Clinical Tales.* New York: Summit Books, 1985.

Serebriakoff, Victor. *Mensa: The Society for the Highly Intelligent.* New York: Stein & Day, 1985.

Siegel, Ronald K. *Intoxication: Life in Pursuit of Artificial Paradise.* New York: E. P. Dutton, 1989.

Silverstein, Alvin, and Virginia B. Silverstein. *Epilepsy.* Edited by J. Gordon Millichap. Philadelphia: J. B. Lippincott, 1975.

Slung, Michele. *The Absent-Minded Professor's Memory Book.* New York: Random House, Ballantine Books, 1985.

Smith, Anthony. *The Mind.* New York: Viking Press, 1984.

Smith, Steven B. *The Great Mental Calculators.* New York: Columbia University Press, 1983.

Springer, Sally P., and Georg Deutsch. *Left Brain, Right Brain.* San Francisco: W. H. Freeman, 1981.

Stanislavski, Constantin. *An Actor Prepares.* Translated by Elizabeth Reynolds Hapgood. New York: Theatre Arts Books, 1979.

Storr, Anthony:
Churchill's Black Dog, Kafka's Mice, and Other Phenomena of the Human Mind. New York: Grove Press, 1988.
Solitude: A Return to the Self. New York: Macmillan, Free Press, 1988.

Taylor, Gordon Rattray. *The Natural History of the Mind.* New York: E. P. Dutton, 1979.

Tredgold, A. F. *Mental Deficiency.* London: Baillière, Tindall & Cox, 1908.

Treffert, Darold A. *Extraordinary People: Understanding "Idiot Savants."* New York: Harper & Row, 1989.

Wallace, Amy. *The Prodigy.* New York: E. P. Dutton, 1986.

Weisberg, Robert. *Creativity: Genius and Other Myths.* New York: W. H. Freeman, 1986.

Wheeler, K. M. *The Creative Mind in Coleridge's Poetry.* Cambridge, Mass.: Harvard University Press, 1981.

Who's Who in the United Nations and Related Agencies. New York: Arno Press, 1975.

Yepsen, Roger B., Jr. *How to Boost Your Brain Power: Achieving Peak Intelligence, Memory and Creativity.* Emmaus, Pa.: Rodale Press, 1987.

Zusne, Leonard, and Warren H. Jones. *Anomalistic Psychology: A Study of Magical Thinking* (2nd ed.). Hillsdale, N.J.: Lawrence Erlbaum Associates, 1989.

Periodicals

Abramson, Arthur S. "The Phantom Phenomenon: Its Use and Disuse." *Bulletin of the New York Academy of Medicine,* March 1981.

Acuna, Armando. "Computer Hacker with a Genius IQ Chooses Street Life." *Los Angeles Times,* March 19, 1989.

"After Two Centuries, Austria's Child Prodigy Has Become the World's Favorite Composer." *People Weekly,* December 28, 1981.

Alper, Joseph. "Our Dual Memory." *Science 86,* July-August 1986.

Associated Press. "Memory: It Seems a Whiff of Chocolate Helps." *New York Times,* July 10, 1990.

"At Last, Medicine Really Listens to Van Gogh." *New York Times,* July 25, 1990.

Barzun, Jacques. "The Paradoxes of Creativity." *The American Scholar,* Summer 1989.

Begley, Sharon. "The Fossils of Language." *Newsweek,* March 15, 1982.

Benderly, Beryl Lieff. "Dialogue of the Deaf." *Psychology Today,* October 1980.

Blakeslee, Sandra. "The Return of the Mind." *American Health,* March 1989.

Bower, Bruce:
"Epileptic PET Probes." *Science News,* April 30, 1988.
"Flashbulb Memories: The Picture Fades." *Science News,* June 1988.

"Brain Under Seizure." *Discover,* August 1988.

Browne, Malcolm W. "Mathematicians Turn to Prose in an Effort to Remember Pi." *Washington Post,* June 18, 1989.

Christon, Lawrence:
"Kim, the Savant Who Came to Hollywood." *Los Angeles Times,* January 8, 1989.
"The Original Rain Man: 'We Got It All . . .' "

Los Angeles Times, March 30, 1989.

"Computerized Biofeedback Training Aids in Spinal Injury Rehabilitation." *JAMA*, February 22, 1985.

"The Creative Virtues of Loneliness." *U.S. News & World Report*, September 12, 1988.

Dusenbury, Delwin, and Franklin H. Knower. "Experimental Studies of the Symbolism of Action and Voice—II." *Quarterly Journal of Speech*, February 1939.

Fay, Martha. "The Piano Is Eddie's Key." *Life*, April 1989.

Flynn, James R. "Massive IQ Gains in 14 Nations: What IQ Tests Really Measure." *Psychological Bulletin*, 1987, Vol. 101, no. 2.

Forbes, Maxwell. "The Mysterious Savant Syndrome." *Pursuit*, First Quarter 1986.

Freeman, Don. "Dr. Seuss from Then to Now." *San Diego Magazine*, May 1986.

Garelik, Glenn. "Are the Progeny Prodigies?" *Discover*, October 1985.

Gladwell, Malcolm. "Why, in Some Fields, Do Early Achievers Seem to Be the Only Kind?" *Washington Post*, April 16, 1990.

Goleman, Daniel. "Major Personality Study Finds that Traits Are Mostly Inherited." *New York Times*, December 2, 1986.

Grove, Valerie. "The Making of a 12-Year-Old Genius." *The Standard*, July 19, 1984.

Haber, Ralph Norman. "Eidetic Images Are Not Just Imaginary." *Psychology Today*, November 1980.

Hamblin, Dora Jane. "They Are 'Idiot Savants'—Wizards of the Calendar." *Life*, March 18, 1966.

Harmetz, Aljean. "Math Stars in a Movie." *New York Times*, March 20, 1988.

Hellerstein, David. "Plotting a Theory of the Brain." *New York Times Magazine*, May 22, 1988.

Holden, Constance. "Creativity and the Troubled Mind." *Psychology Today*, April 1987.

Holland, Bernard. "A Man Who Sees What Others Hear." *New York Times*, November 19, 1981.

Horn, Jack C. "Relax, You'll Run Faster." *Psychology Today*, January-February 1989.

Horwitz, William A., et al. "Identical Twin-'Idiot Savants'-Calendar Calculators." *American Journal of Psychiatry*, 1965, Vol. 121, p. 1075.

"Inside Einstein's Brain." *Science 85*, March 1985.

Jankovic, Joseph, and J. Peter Glass. "Metoclopramide-Induced Phantom Dyskinesia." *Neurology*, March 1985.

Kanner, Bernice. "From the Subliminal to the Ridiculous." *New York Times*, December 4, 1989.

Kendall, John. "A Report on Japan's Phenomenal Young Violinists." *Violins and Violinists*, November-December 1959.

Kolata, Gina. "Studying Learning in the Womb." *Science*, July 20, 1984.

Krajick, Kevin. "Sound Too Good to Be True?:

Behind the Boom in Subliminal Tapes." *Newsweek*, July 30, 1990.

Kupferberg, Herbert. "A Seussian Celebration." *Parade Magazine*, February 26, 1984.

LaPlante, Eve. "The Riddle of TLE." *Atlantic*, November 1988.

Lauerman, Connie. "Scale." *Chicago Tribune*, February 4, 1990.

Lidz, Franz. "It's Mind over Matter, 2-0." *Sports Illustrated*, October 30, 1989.

"Life of Jedediah Buxton." *Gentleman's Magazine*, June 1754.

Loehr, Jim. "The Mental Game: Seeing Is Believing." *World Tennis*, March 1989.

Lord, Lewis J., et al. "The Brain Battle." *U.S. News & World Report*, January 19, 1987.

Lumsden, Charles J., and Edward O. Wilson. "The Relation between Biological and Cultural Evolution." *Journal of Social Biological Structure*, 1985, Vol. 8, pp. 343-359.

"Maths Genius, 11, Starts Degree Course." *The Independent*, November 19, 1990.

"Mind over Matter." *Discover*, August 1990.

Montgomery, Geoffrey. "Molecules of Memory." *Discover*, December 1989.

Morgenstern, Joe. "Robin Williams." *New York Times Magazine*, November 11, 1990.

Morris, Scot. "Brainbuster: Omni's New I.Q. Test." *Omni*, July 1981.

"New Images, New Insights into Your Brain." *Psychology Today*, November 1988.

Ogintz, Eileen. "Torchbearer." *Chicago Tribune*, August 10, 1988.

Raeburn, Paul. "Memory Tea." *American Health*, January-February 1990.

Read, Gerald H. "The Akademgorodok of Novosibirsk." *Intellect*, October 1972.

"Read Any Good Records Lately?" *Time*, January 4, 1982.

Reich, Howard. "Rosalyn Tureck Reprising Her Career." *Chicago Tribune*, January 18, 1990.

Reid, T. R. "The Man with the Endless Memory." *Washington Post*, June 18, 1989.

Roach, Mary. "Unlikely Genius." *Hippocrates*, May-June 1989.

Roberts, Marjory. "Flashbulb Memories: Fade to Black." *Psychology Today*, June 1988.

Robotham, Rosemarie. "Islands of Genius: Mind." *Omni*, September 1989.

Runco, Mark A., and Michael D. Bahleda. "Birth-Order and Divergent Thinking." *Journal of Genetic Psychology*, 1986, Vol. 148, pp. 119-125.

"Ruth Routs Left." *Daily Mail*, February 28, 1984.

Schrage, Michael. "Are Ideas Viruses of the Mind?" *Washington Post*, October 30, 1988.

"Secret Voices: Messages That Manipulate." *Time*, September 10, 1979.

Sherman, Richard A., and Crystal J. Sherman. "Prevalence and Characteristics of Chronic Phantom Limb Pain among American Veterans." *American Journal of Physical Medicine*, October 1983.

Sternhell, Carol. "Bellow's Typewriters and Other Tics of the Trade." *New York Times*, September 2, 1984.

Stratton, George M. "Mnemonic Feat of the 'Shass Pollak'." *Psychological Review*, November 1917.

Stromeyer, Charles F., III. "Eidetikers." *Psychology Today*, November 1970.

Sverdlik, Alan. "Mensa Brings Mind Games South." *Atlanta Constitution*, June 28, 1989.

"This Man Is an Island." *People*, January 22, 1989.

Treffert, Darold A.:
"The Idiot Savant: A Review of the Syndrome." *American Journal of Psychiatry*, May 1988.
"An Unlikely Virtuoso." *The Sciences*, January-February 1988.

Trotter, R. J. "Geschwind's Syndrome: Van Gogh's Malady." *Psychology Today*, November 1985.

"Unbreakable Language Barriers." *Discover*, December 1989.

Waitzkin, Fred. "Kasparov." *New York Times Magazine*, October 7, 1990.

Walters, Mark J. "The Soul of a Prodigy." *Reader's Digest*, March 1987.

Webster, Bayard. "She Does Cube Roots in Her Head." *New York Times*, November 10, 1976.

Weisburd, Stefi. "Eat to Remember." *Science News*, May 23, 1987.

Witelson, Sandra F. "Hand and Sex Differences in the Isthmus and Genu of the Human Corpus Callosum." *Brain*, 1989, Vol. 112, pp. 799-835.

"Wizard of 0000s." *Life*, February 18, 1952.

Wood, Daniel B.:
"His Equation Works for Inner-City Kids." *Chicago Tribune*, April 26, 1988.
"In City Kids He Finds the Mathematician's Mind." *Christian Science Monitor*, March 24, 1988.

Yagoda, Ben. "American Writers in Paris." *Horizon*, November 1980.

Yarnell, Philip R., and Steve Lynch. "The 'Ding': Amnestic States in Football Trauma." *Neurology*, February 1973.

Zajonc, R. B., and Gregory B. Markus. "Birth Order and Intellectual Development." *Psychological Review*, 1975, Vol. 82, no. 1.

Other Sources

Alzheimer's Disease and Related Disorders. Pamphlet. Chicago, Ill.: Alzheimer's Disease and Related Disorders Association, 1987.

Memory and Aging. Pamphlet. Chicago, Ill.: Alzheimer's Disease and Related Disorders Association, 1987.

Weinstein, Sidney, Robert J. Vetter, and Eugene A. Sersen. *Physiological and Experiential Concomitants of the Phantom.* Project Report, Grant RD-427, Vocational Rehabilitation Administration. New York: Department of Rehabilitation Medicine, Albert Einstein College of Medicine, June 1959-May 1964.

Index

Numerals in italics indicate an illustration of the subject mentioned.

Time-Life Books is a division of Time Life Inc.,
a wholly owned subsidiary of
THE TIME INC. BOOK COMPANY

TIME-LIFE BOOKS

Managing Editor: Thomas H. Flaherty
Director of Editorial Resources:
Elise D. Ritter-Clough
Director of Photography and Research:
John Conrad Weiser
Editorial Board: Dale M. Brown, Roberta Conlan,
Laura Foreman, Lee Hassig, Jim Hicks,
Blaine Marshall, Rita Thievon Mullin, Henry
Woodhead

PUBLISHER: Joseph J. Ward

Associate Publisher: Ann Mirabito
Editorial Director: Russell B. Adams, Jr.
Marketing Director: Anne C. Everhart
Director of Design: Louis Klein
Production Manager: Prudence G. Harris
Supervisor of Quality Control: James King

Editorial Operations
Production: Celia Beattie
Library: Louise D. Forstall
Computer Composition: Deborah G. Tait (Manager),
Monika D. Thayer, Janet Barnes Syring,
Lillian Daniels

Library of Congress
Cataloging-in-Publication Data
The Mystifying mind / by the editors of Time-Life
Books.
p. cm. (Library of curious and unusual facts).
Includes bibliographical references.
ISBN 0-8094-7707-6 (trade)
ISBN 0-8094-7708-4 (lib. bdg.)
1. Intellect. 2. Genius. 3. Neuropsychology.
4. Brain.
I. Time-Life Books. II. Series.
BF431.M86 1991
150—dc20   90-24843 CIP

LIBRARY OF CURIOUS AND UNUSUAL FACTS

SERIES EDITOR: Laura Foreman
Series Administrator: Roxie France-Nuriddin
Art Director: Susan K. White
Picture Editor: Sally Collins

Editorial Staff for *The Mystifying Mind*
Text Editor: Carl A. Posey
Associate Editors/Research: Debra Diamond Smit
(principal), Susan E. Arritt
Assistant Editor/Research: Ruth J. Moss
Assistant Art Director: Alan Pitts
Senior Copy Coordinators: Jarelle S. Stein (princi-
pal), Anthony K. Pordes
Picture Coordinator: Jennifer Iker
Editorial Assistant: Terry Ann Paredes

Special Contributors: Joe Alper, Eliot Marshall,
Peter Pocock, George Russell, Chuck Smith (text);
Maureen McHugh, Tanya Nádas-Taylor, Eugenia S.
Scharf (research); Hazel Blumberg-McKee
(index)

Correspondents: Elisabeth Kraemer-Singh (Bonn),
Christine Hinze (London), Christina Lieberman (New
York), Maria Vincenza Aloisi (Paris), Ann Natanson
(Rome).
Valuable assistance was also provided by Angelika
Lemmer (Bonn); Judy Aspinall (London); Elizabeth
Brown, Katheryn White (New York); Ann Wise
(Rome); Dick Berry, Mieko Ikeda (Tokyo).

The Consultants:
William R. Corliss, the general consultant for the
series, is a physicist-turned-writer who has spent the
last twenty-five years compiling collections of
anomalies in the fields of geophysics, geology, ar-
chaeology, astronomy, biology, and psychology. He
has written about science and technology for NASA,
the National Science Foundation, and the Energy
Research and Development Administration (among
others). Mr. Corliss is also the author of more than
thirty books on scientific mysteries, including *Mysterious Universe, The Unfathomed Mind,* and *Handbook of Unusual Natural Phenomena.*

Dr. Richard Restak, the overall consultant for the
book, is an associate professor of neurology at the
Georgetown University School of Medicine and a
neurologist and neuropsychiatrist with a private
practice in Washington, D.C. He is the author of six
best-selling books: *Premeditated Man,* chosen by
the *New York Times* as one of the Notable Books of
1975; *The Brain: The Last Frontier; The Self-
Seekers; The Mind; The Brain;* and *The Infant Mind.*
He also contributes a column to *Newsday* and
serves on the Advisory Council to the National Foundation for Brain Research.

Marcello Truzzi, a professor of sociology at Eastern
Michigan University, is director of the Center for
Scientific Anomalies Research (CSAR) and editor of
its journal, *Zetetic Scholar.*

TIME ®
LIFE
BOOKS